TALES OF TERROR'S
HORROR MOVIES OF THE MILLENNIUM
2020
20 YEARS OF FEAR

HORROR MOVIES *of the* MILLENNIUM

20 YEARS OF FEAR

STEVE HUTCHISON

FEATURING

STEVE HUTCHISON

CRITIC

First Printing: 2020
ISBN-13: 979-8622785924

Bookstores and wholesalers: Please contact books@terror.ca.

Tales of Terror
tales@terror.ca
www.terror.ca

INTRODUCTION

Included in this book are reviews of the 5 best horror films for each year between 2000 and 2019, and reviews of the top 10 horror movies released in the same period.

Each entry includes a picture of the antagonist, a star rating, a synopsis, and a three-paragraph review.

CONTENTS

TOP 10 HORROR MOVIES OF THE MILLENNIUM

SAW
2004

8/8

Chained to pipes in a disused bathroom, two men are given a puzzle to which they must provide answers.

Saw is both a torture film and a police procedural. It's a ongoing mystery that explores new grounds in storytelling. It's refreshing and unique, yet closely reminiscent of the Cube franchise and Se7en. The power of this movie resides in how it cleverly parses clues, how complex the puzzle is, and how twists and turns reveal themselves. They do so in the most creatively shocking fashion.

The writing is brilliant. The photography is impeccable. Extreme color balance, photo filters and quick editing gives this movie a particular trademark. The actors do a fine job of keeping us guessing, sympathizing, cringing. Their performances make you feel as powerless as their characters become. One of the two main plot lines happens in one place and with only two characters.

While the cast is limited, each of their movements, lines and performances has been scrutinized and polished. When dialogue makes room for gore, Saw shows another significant strength; displaying pain and suffering crudely and realistically, thanks to stunning top-of-the line effects. Innovative, yet formulaic, Saw gives us a new horror icon with its own sonata; a nod to slasher flicks.

EVIL DEAD
2013

8/8

Tricked into a week-end of rehab in a remote cabin by her friends, a girl in withdrawal believes she is surrounded by demons.

Technically second remake of a 1981 revolutionary cult classic, this movie has one of the strongest horror fan bases in history and a new generation of teenagers to seduce. The purists might bump on a few details, but none of the franchise's gimmicks have been overlooked and the movie looks like a million bucks. The gore effects are incredibly realistic and are torture even to the audience.

Bruce Campbell's Ash isn't part of the story, but his design and wit are found across the production. The performances range from forgettable to awesome, and it seems to be what the producers were after. This was also true of all previous films. Some actors hold back because the script wants them to until they get their special moment, at which point they unleash their true talent.

From photography to the narrative, every aspect of Evil Dead is calculated. It knows how to scare, disgust and make you jump, and does so with perfect timing. Humor is limited, much like the original Evil Dead. The biggest shift in tone between this and the first two is in the polish and the technology at hand. Nothing is left to chance. Expect twists and Easter eggs from beginning to end.

ΙΤ
2017

8/8
A group of bullied kids band together against a shapeshifting demon clown.

Keep away from children! This film is not for them, despite the fact that all protagonists are tweens. They're young but they're in a horror movie and they're here to suffer. As such, they get beaten in the cruelest ways. For a while, the script opposes each child in the "losers' club" to Pennywise, one of the creepiest clowns in film history. He fucks with them then leaves, often interrupted.

Perfect sound, pacing, lighting, perfect acting and overall cinematography; It is nearly flawless. It is quite simply one of the best horror movies ever made, and, undoubtedly, one of the scariest. In comparison with the 1990 mini-series by the same title, everything, here, is more extreme, sad, scary and shocking. You get a bunch of solid jump scares that fool you even if you expect them.

Many special effects are computer generated and that's not really a problem. It's a style. Complaining about the abundance of compositing would be nitpicking. The characters' chemistry is representative of the actors' bounding on set. Their relationships are warm and compelling. The adults are all scums. This is the first part of a duology and it takes place in the 1980s.

IT: CHAPTER TWO
2019

8/8

Twenty-seven years after defeating a supernatural being, six friends are reunited to kill it once and for all.

This is the kind of film non-horror movie fans think we watch all the time. If only they knew! A phenomenon like It: Chapter 2 happens once every year, at best, and is just as good as Part 1 was. The casting is brilliant. It takes a while to figure out who's who, between the cast of Part 1 and their adult counterpart, but it eventually sinks in. I ended up connecting with everyone in this.

There are several flashbacks, so the original cast reprise their roles. Pennywise returns, too, of course, to fuck with everyone's mind and kill a few. There are genuinely creepy moments that will make you swallow your tongue. The creature design is unbelievable. This is a horror fan's wet dream come true. I was one with this movie and never wanted it to end.

This story constantly came full circle. When we think of what a quintessential horror movie is, this is the one that comes to mind. The special effects are out of this world. There are jump scares at every turn. There's a bit of every horror trope in this, but with a special touch that makes them unique. Legendary casting! Amazing cinematography! What a great flick!

1408
2007

8/8
A man is trapped inside a hotel room and terrorized by ghosts.

At its purest form, 1408 is a condensed version of The Shining. This is obvious. The film is based on a short story by Stephen King and he can rip off his own material if he feels like it, but is it worth watching? 1408 needs to be considered a stand alone film and appreciated as such. It contains enough fresh material and twists you won't see coming. All in all, this is a great movie. Here's why...

First, it stars John Cusack in one of the best roles of his glorious career. Samuel L. Jackson is there to shuffle the deck. He wants to help, he's friendly, yet he's ominous. This is one of the most claustrophobic horror movies ever made. It's basically about a man stuck in a hotel room from another dimension. He should be surrounded by people and traffic, yet he couldn't be more isolated.

The acting is irreproachable. The limited set and cast are an advantage. Horror is mostly psychological, here, and it will send shivers down your spine on many occasions. One of 1408's creepiest cards is making your imagination wander. Exactly how far does room 1408's reach extends? At what point, in the film, does the haunting start? The more you think, the scarier this film gets...

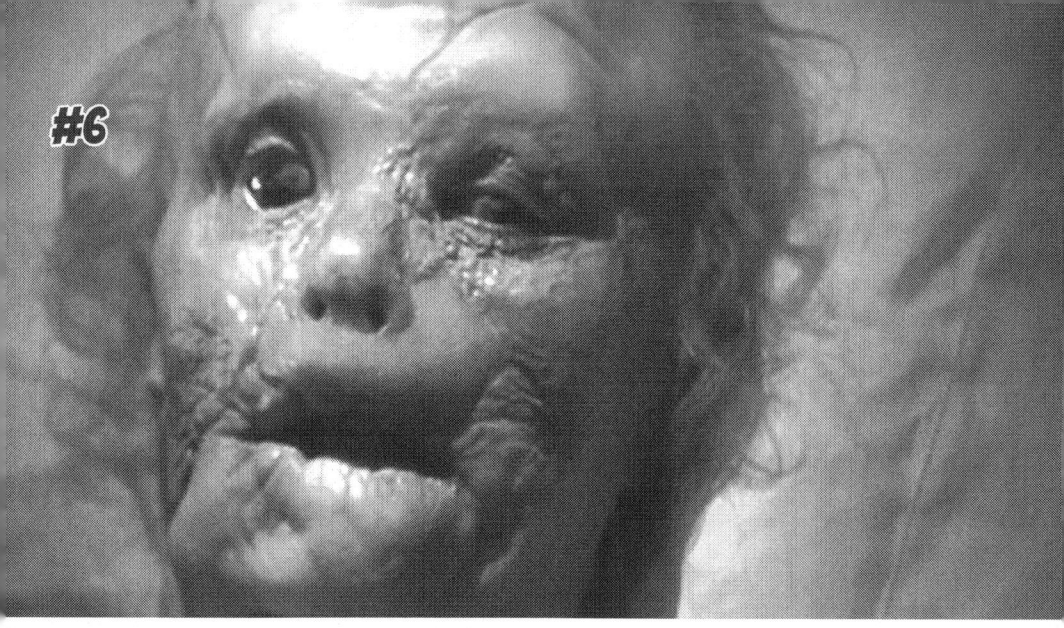

HANNIBAL
2001

8/8

A runaway cannibal is tracked down by the police and a past victim of his.

Anthony Hopkins approached the Hannibal persona with subtlety, class, vocabulary and calm in 1991's Silence of the Lambs. His passivity was concerning and he was frightening by implication only until the third act. He was a mysterious figure in the shadow of another; both a protagonist and an antagonist to Jodie Foster's character. She is replaced by Julianne Moore in this sequel.

Though her absence breaks an otherwise clean continuity; with references to the past and recognizable patterns, Moore fills the mandate with a fair rendition of Clarice Starling. This is Hopkins' show, regardless. The gore is glorified but celebrated by slow captivating build-up that pays off. The film is eerie, looks luxurious and the score gives significant gravitas to suspense.

It borrows from the cheesiest horror subgenres yet benefits from a good budget, stunning make-up, keen photography and the best actors money can rent. The end result is highly professional, calculated and always reaches full impact. Hannibal appears omniscient, as he always did, and his intelligence is terrifying when fully exposed. He is both who we follow and who we fear.

11.22.63
2016

8/8
A time traveler attempts to prevent John F. Kennedy's assassination.

Who has never felt the deep desire to fix today's problems yesterday; to go back in time and erase critical mistakes. The film explores this question more in-depth than Back to the Future did. 11.22.63 is easily one of the best time travelling stories ever adapted to screen. It's a mini-series, so it requires involvement, but every second is worth it. You should jump in head first!

11.22.63 is a science-fiction story and a supernatural drama. It contains horrific scenes, but in the midst of it evolves a touching love story. This is also one of Stephen King's most political tale, and one of his most mature work despite the colorful premise. In this mini-series, a time traveler; James Franco's character, attempts to prevent John F. Kennedy's assassination in 1963.

This feature is dialogue-oriented. Though not everyone is a big star, all actors are highly competent. Those who are reluctant to see James Franco in the protagonist's shoes will surely reconsider. He is amusing and extremely sympathetic. His character deserves to achieves his goals but fails at every step. You see, the past doesn't want to be changed. The past is the ultimate villain, in fact...

THE OTHERS
2001

8/8

The mother of two photosensitive children becomes convinced that her house is haunted.

This is the kind of film you want to watch in one streak, without interruption and in the right mood, because subsequent viewing won't be as impactful. A lot of this production resides in its surprises, scattered here and there, and in its twists. The Others will definitely become your go-to movie about ghosts for its quintessence and its haunting atmosphere.

Nicole Kidman deserves praise for her acting. She's not playing your run-of-the-mill mother. First, this is a period piece. Second, she's isolated in the middle of nowhere. Third, her husband is at war. Fourth, her kids are weird. There is more to this character than meets the eye. We know this because the first shot of the movie presents her in a state of panic. Her character never gets better.

Every word, in The Others, has a meaning. Alejandro Amenábar, writer, director and musician, shows you what he thinks you should see. His film is slow but surprisingly dense. The cast and sets are limited, but the film looks like a million bucks. It is visually rich, it is immersive and it's scary as hell. Also, all the actors, even the young ones, do a bang-up job.

THE BUTTERFLY EFFECT
2004

7/8

A man afflicted by a supernatural disease learns to travel back in the past to make the present better.

The Butterfly Effect is a tragic supernatural thriller that deals with time travel in its own creative way using a logic we haven't seen before. Its main protagonist, Ashton Kutcher's character, uses passages from private journals he wrote to revisit his youth and alter the past to make the present better; better for him, his friend and his love interest.

The film deals with difficult subjects like pedophilia, violence, bad parenting, mental illness, physical disability, suffering and death. It is a story about regrets and remorse, of things we would've done differently had we known the consequences of our acts. Despite and implausible plot, this movie is extremely sad, very serious and highly introspective.

And, aside its complex concept, the script doesn't have major plot holes. For such a tragic story, it even has its fun moments. The writing is fine, the directing irreproachable, and the actors are so good they make us forget we're watching fiction. This movie passes by so fast it leaves us wanting more. The gimmick is poignant and strangely addicting.

TRICK 'R TREAT
2007

7/8
A Halloween night turns into a blood bath for different groups of people connected to each other.

This is one of the best horror anthology films ever made. It is right up there with Creepshow and Trilogy of Terror. It sets itself apart from the norm by the way it intertwines 6 segments. Things happen before, during and after another, and we're never sure in which order. The script is brilliantly layered in a way to juxtapose stories seamlessly. Michael Dougherty orchestrates this like a king.

The photography is so precise and so optimized that Dougherty earns our attention from frame one. The scary parts are scary, the build-up is outstanding, the gore striking, the stories original and the twists surprising. Gore feels real and so does the rest of the effects. Trick 'r Treat's major flaw is that its tales feel incomplete despite an intention to innovate with a new kind of narrative.

Story 1 doesn't stand on its own but sets the tone nicely. Story 2 is about a man who gives a kid poisoned candy. Story 3 follows a bunch of teenagers who play a prank on a friend. Story 4 is about a special party in a remote location. Story 5 introduces a small demonic character who will teach a hermit a lesson. This is the best story in the pack. Story 6 ties the last lose ends nicely.

BEST HORROR MOVIES OF 2000

HOLLOW MAN
2000

7/8

A scientist turned invisible by a newly discovered potion becomes a threat for his colleagues.

Watch Kevin Bacon lose his mind in ways only he can in a superior horror thriller directed by the great Paul Verhoeven. Elisabeth Shue plays the love interest and the protagonist. She is the ideal ex-girlfriend and a perfect fit for the role. Hollow Man is the classic story of a rushed scientific experiment gone wrong, but with a huge budget invested in big names and special effects.

In this unofficial remake of The Invisible Man, Bacon becomes increasingly unstable and violent. This is a remarkable thriller when it is tense, an excellent horror movie when it is violent and enthralling science fiction otherwise. The metamorphosis sequences are stellar. We get to see complex and somewhat realistic 3-D renders of the whole transformation from opacity to transparency and back.

The actors are on top of their game. The film wouldn't work without their chemistry. They make use believe in what they see despite the green screens and color keying. They have a plausible love and hate dynamic, a past and a present, conflicts and friendships. Despite the fantastic elements they deal with, their dialogue is mature and right out of a 90's titillating thriller. This is a must see!

FINAL DESTINATION
2000

7/8

Death comes back at a medium who saved his classmates' life and his own after a premonition.

Final Destination's supernatural serial killer is slow, invisible, strategic and angry. It is an ill-defined force that answers to specific rules only talented writers could come up and juggle with. It's a character that doesn't need to be recast in sequels and therefore has the potential to generate an infinite franchise. It is a frightening villain because you can't kill it; let alone touch it.

The performances are authentic, energetic and supported by strong dialogue. In real life, "signs" are reserved for the crazy who see meaning in the smallest details and who connect dots where there are none. Devon Sawa's character is patronized for it, making him the default geek and some guy no one believes. While this is a recurring horror cliché, here it feels natural, logical, pertinent.

This is one of the smartest and most eccentric gimmicks of modern horror movie history. Imagine an intangible telekinetic force that slowly shapes events, mistakes and catastrophes to its advantage and aligns them in a way to assault the same person iteratively; making sure they are dead before dealing with the next victim. Other details are handled by a spoon-fed but entertaining procedural.

GINGER SNAPS
2000

7/8

A teenager bitten by a werewolf undergoes slow metamorphosis.

To be terrifying, a werewolf movie needs to have its protagonist be afflicted by the curse and not be mere victim of the beast itself. Apprehending the transformation represents half the fear there is to be had in this subgenre and Ginger Snaps is excellent at it. It offers a teenage but not cute girly spin on the typical formula and goes as far as metaphorizing puberty in the werewolf equation.

The use of 3-D animation isn't abusive and most of the good stuff relies on practical effects, fortunately. The visual are always frightening and lit just right, though more of the beast should have been shown. The film looks good but can't afford showing it all. It would rather redeem itself with a strong script and performances that win you over, given character development is your thing.

Werewolves were never this sexy. Katharine Isabelle is a violent and sexualized version of 1985's Teen Wolf's coming of age rendition; proof that times have changed. Humor, sensuality and horror find a perfect balance in the hands of Karen Walton and John Fawcett who flesh out a tragic monster evolving from protagonist to antagonist over a few days and who can titillate us as well as scare us.

SCREAM 3
2000

7/8

A copycat killer decimates the cast and crew of a popular horror movie based on actual events.

Scream gets a little more grandiose, graciously moving its plot and its survivors to Hollywood. The main protagonists are adults, now, and they have been through a lot. The tone is consequentially dark, but spiced up by the re-introduction of stereotypical characters and surreal settings. The action mostly takes place on the set of a film inspired by the events of the two first Scream movies.

By tradition, the new faces are either used as slasher meat, red herrings or both. Guessing the killer's identity is harder than ever, the characters having been left underdeveloped and the amount of speaking roles having increased. Scream purists will find the script clustered, superficial, and cold when it comes to dialogue. This one isn't big on details and human chemistry.

The previous film was a self-referential sequel; the third one focuses on the rules of trilogies. The game, then, becomes to second-guess the outcome, based on our personal fandom knowledge or hints left by the franchise, so far. As stated in Scream 3, for better or worse, anything goes in this one. It won't rub everybody the right way, but it's still a brilliantly directed high-budget slasher.

AMERICAN PSYCHO
2000

7/8
A wealthy investment banking executive grows increasingly insane.

American Psycho introduces a protagonist who is both charming and despicable. Through his thoughts and actions, we understand he is a sociopath who will stop at nothing to shape the world as he sees fit. He is on the brink of a psychosis and we watch him regress with delight. He has no respect for women and is obsessively competitive towards men. Here's a one-way ticket into his madness...

This is a satire on the late 1980s and its yuppies. It takes place in Manhattan in all its glory. Patrick Bateman, the lead, hangs out in trendy restaurants that serve meals so pretentious they seem out of a fairy tale. The movie is sexy, kinky, and features both male and female nudity. It also contains one of the most legendary threesomes in film history!

The structure is unusual. Bateman's antagonist, a detective, is a stress factor but isn't much of a threat. Consequences to his murders are somehow inexistent, it seems, and his true enemy is his insanity, as it turns out. The social commentary is strong, yet you could miss it if you're not looking deep enough. American Psycho is a mainstream jewel and an instant classic.

BEST HORROR MOVIES OF 2001

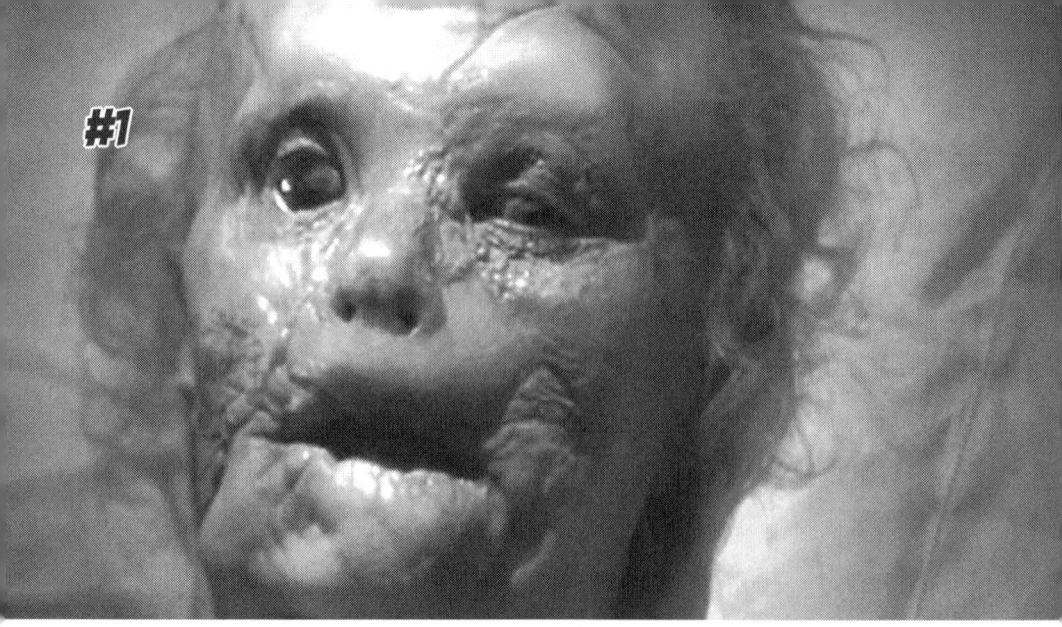

HANNIBAL
2001

8/8
A runaway cannibal is tracked down by the police and a past victim of his.

Anthony Hopkins approached the Hannibal persona with subtlety, class, vocabulary and calm in 1991's Silence of the Lambs. His passivity was concerning and he was frightening by implication only until the third act. He was a mysterious figure in the shadow of another; both a protagonist and an antagonist to Jodie Foster's character. She is replaced by Julianne Moore in this sequel.

Though her absence breaks an otherwise clean continuity; with references to the past and recognizable patterns, Moore fills the mandate with a fair rendition of Clarice Starling. This is Hopkins' show, regardless. The gore is glorified but celebrated by slow captivating build-up that pays off. The film is eerie, looks luxurious and the score gives significant gravitas to suspense.

It borrows from the cheesiest horror subgenres yet benefits from a good budget, stunning make-up, keen photography and the best actors money can rent. The end result is highly professional, calculated and always reaches full impact. Hannibal appears omniscient, as he always did, and his intelligence is terrifying when fully exposed. He is both who we follow and who we fear.

THE OTHERS
2001

8/8

The mother of two photosensitive children becomes convinced that her house is haunted.

This is the kind of film you want to watch in one streak, without interruption and in the right mood, because subsequent viewing won't be as impactful. A lot of this production resides in its surprises, scattered here and there, and in its twists. The Others will definitely become your go-to movie about ghosts for its quintessence and its haunting atmosphere.

Nicole Kidman deserves praise for her acting. She's not playing your run-of-the-mill mother. First, this is a period piece. Second, she's isolated in the middle of nowhere. Third, her husband is at war. Fourth, her kids are weird. There is more to this character than meets the eye. We know this because the first shot of the movie presents her in a state of panic. Her character never gets better.

Every word, in The Others, has a meaning. Alejandro Amenábar, writer, director and musician, shows you what he thinks you should see. His film is slow but surprisingly dense. The cast and sets are limited, but the film looks like a million bucks. It is visually rich, it is immersive and it's scary as hell. Also, all the actors, even the young ones, do a bang-up job.

THE HOLE
2001

7/8

Four teenagers uncover and explore the depths of a sealed underground bomb shelter.

The Hole is at times poignant, frustrating, disturbing, but there is more, here, than meets the eye. This is a legendary mindfuck. The story is simple enough, but it gets increasingly layered the deeper we get. Parallel to the main timeline is a psychiatric investigation. This leads to one of the most powerful twists in the history of horror films and it happens sooner than you'd think.

Things gets very sinister passed a certain point. The teenagers realize they are locked inside the bunker they were partying in. Claustrophobia ensues. All this happens while the main protagonist, played by Thora Birch shows her unrequited love for Mike, one of two jocks, played by Desmond Harrington. Keira Knightley plays the hot chick and Laurence Fox her fling. All four are exceptional!

We get a good understanding of who everybody is, and they all react appropriately through the obstacles ahead. They are not exactly stereotypes; they remind us of people we know. They remind us of us. This film has a great kick, but it particularly stands out because of how shocking it gets. The suspenseful score makes everything better, and what an immersive bomb shelter set!

FRAILTY

2001

7/8

A man confesses to an FBI agent that his father's visions led to a series of murders.

Fifteen minutes in, the hook is introduced. And there you have it, a father recruiting his kids in a demon hunt. He's having visions, so he's either psychotic or blessed by God. The difference between magic and mental illness is what everyone else sees. The father, played by Bill Paxton in one of his best roles, involves his two kids in his madness. The oldest one doesn't like it one bit...

The kids are played by young Matt O'Leary and Jeremy Sumpter. We instantly buy them as brothers. Adult Adam, one of them, is played by Matthew McConaughey, years later, who retells to an FBI agent what is pretty much a period piece to us. The main timeline takes place in 1979, when people still had simple lives; before the internet and satellite television. It's also when we stopped praying.

This is a brutal film, but the violence is not particularly graphic. A lot is accomplished through clever, tight editing. Sound effects account for a lot when it comes to implicit pain. Frailty is kind of slow, but well-paced. The suspense constantly rises until it reaches an amazing third act that you won't soon forget. This one will make you question your faith, or lack thereof...

JOY RIDE
2001

7/8
A truck driver torments two brothers who pranked him.

Joy Ride is, without a doubt, one of the best road movies out there. It is flawlessly written and transposed to screen by the keen eyes of experienced cinematographers. It lengthily exposes three likable protagonists played by Steve Zahn, Paul Walker and Leelee Sobieski. Their performance is authentic and layered. They are the boys and girls next door.

J.J.Abrams and Clay Tarver lay out a simple synopsis and stick to it; the way old films used to. It's a horror film so it gets tempted by the supernatural but prefers the subtlety of surrealism. It is a perfect companion piece to 1971's Duel and 1986's The Hitcher. This peculiar formula has been tested before and never gets tired, given the ambiance is dense enough and the suspense well executed.

This movie succeeds on those levels. What's more, a road movie typically involves car chases and stunts which this one pulls off incredibly well. The killer's truck looks mean; filmed with calculated framing and movement and in angles meant to scare and alienate. Even the action scenes are darker than heroic. As a bonus, horror movie fans get a new marketable horror villain called "Rusty Nail".

BEST HORROR MOVIES OF 2002

CABIN FEVER
2002

7/8

Isolated in a cabin in the woods, a group of friends become infected by a fast spreading disease.

If Cabin Fever at first behaves like any horror movie taking place in a remote cottage, it in fact finds its identity in that the main threat is an infectious disease. It starts simply enough with friends, including couples, seemingly supportive of each other but, then, traitors to each other when in jeopardy. The actors do a fine job with a vacillating script and sometimes odd dialogue.

The humor, here, is somewhat derived of inside jokes that we don't always fully get. It's a style, but it's consequently amateurish in its presentation. Paranoia, isolation and contagion are the fears the film plays on, and it's excellent at it. Between what you see, what is suggested and what you imagine, gore reminds you that this isn't just a psychological thriller.

The disease spreads so fast that it is played for a cringe and a laugh. By its raging scope, the plague is depicted as some impersonal slasher icon, with proper pacing, structure and body count. The sets, the score and the photo are reminiscent of similar subgenres, but, under this lens, the material is fresh enough on its own to generate something unique, entertaining, funny and sinister.

DOG SOLDIERS
2002

7/8
A routine military exercise in the wilderness turns into a nightmare.

Werewolf movies are rarely just about werewolves. They often belong to one or several other subgenres, perhaps to tell a bigger story. Dog Soldier is no exception. It is the Predator and Night of the Living Dead rendition of a werewolf flick. It features British soldiers on a training mission. They're tough guys with guns stuck in the middle of the woods. This story pretty much writes itself.

The werewolves are bipeds. We see a lot of them but only in quick shots. They're scary and sure do a lot of damage. They're smart and organized, and aren't apparently allergic to silver. We get three transformation scenes and they're not impressive. They're cheats. That being said, there aren't many lycanthrope films out there, let alone good ones, and this is one of the best.

The actors are good but the characters are generic. They're soldiers, after all. The gore is disgustingly realistic. The film is cold and dark, but contains a healthy dose of humor to lighten things up from one action scene to another. The movie starts with a bang, slows down, but soon picks up the pace, escalates in a crescendo and never let's go. What a ride!

RESIDENT EVIL
2002

7/8

A military unit explores a zombie infested maze controlled by a super computer.

Though it doesn't exactly reflect the video game that it is based on, Resident Evil legitimately feels like one. Its characters are emotionally strong, agile and armed to the teeth. Many are throw-away and the ones we are mainly centering on are amnesic. They are stuck in a maze where they succumb to death one after another in mind-boggling ways; some by zombie bite, some by machines.

The composited zombies could use additional passes, but every other aspect of the aesthetic is spot on. The camera is always where it should be and sometimes beyond. Even seemingly useless close-ups end up revealing hints crucial to the plot. Every frame is studied and the photography is impeccable. We toggle between action and horror with ease, either cheering for the heroes or fearing for them.

At times, the science-fiction facets somewhat saturate the screenplay. Resident Evil is also an adventure film in which the protagonists always move forward without looking back. The story takes place inside a secret laboratory filled with traps, so, as opposed to the original game, we get much more depth than a mere haunted house packed with flesh-eating creatures.

EIGHT LEGGED FREAKS
2002

6/8
A town is being overrun by giant mutated spiders.

Because no other reference comes to mind, I'll call this is a supersized version of Arachnophobia, where everything is bigger, funnier, and more intense. The 3D spiders look fake, but this being a slapstick comedy, we tend to be more forgiving. It's also an action film. It has an incessant pacing and an enthralling score that keeps you on your toes.

Once shit hits the fan, there's no way to stop this thing. It's an epic roller-coaster ride. The deaths are non-lethal, so the gore is minimal. We never get confirmation that anyone dies. This is the kind of film everybody wanted to make and see in the 1950s, but with today's technology. It's an abundance of special effects that weren't possible then.

We get an assortment of colorful actors playing vibrant characters. We're talking David Arquette, Kari Wuhrer, Doug E. Doug, and Scarlett Johansson. The producers trusted inexperienced screenwriter and director Ellory Elkayem with a reasonable budget and he pulled it off nicely. This is a B movie disguised as a blockbuster. It's not for everyone, but it's accessible, nonetheless.

BUBBA HO-TEP
2002

6/8
Two elders fight for their lives in a nursing home haunted by a mummy.

This is a small cast. The film is shot all in one place, backstories aside. Bruce Campbell plays Elvis Presley... or one of his impersonators. The script is never clear about it. Campbell gets the best lines. He's a caricature of himself "with a growth on his pecker". Ossie Davis plays his friend, who thinks he's JFK. A black JFK. As hilarious as this may be, it exposes the sad truth about aging.

Bubba Ho-Tep is a dark comedy, but it has an alarming subtext. The theme of aging in a culture that only values youth is downright depressing. After all, Bruce Campbell is the Elvis Presley of horror fans. Watching him stuck in bed or using a walker to move around is as funny as it is disconcerting. Despite its childish humor, Bubba Ho-Tep is brutally honest.

This is based on a novella by the same name. Sometimes, writer and director Don Coscarelli relies on visions in quick successions to convey the villain's backstory and it doesn't work. It's annoying and it breaks the flow. Elvis' flashbacks, on the other hand, are very amusing. This is a fun film with a cool score that's just right and adds to the ambiance.

BEST HORROR MOVIES OF 2003

FINAL DESTINATION 2
2003

7/8
People saved from a high way pile up by a medium are visited by Death.

Part 1 had a solid script supporting a great gimmick that left people wanting more; serial murders by an invisible force that can be slowed down or postponed but never destroyed. What's more, it was based on the premise that the main protagonist was implicitly psychic. Part 2 makes the most of these foundations and delivers more of what we liked the first time around.

Most sequels suffer from the fact that their lead is traumatized, which often gives the audience no party to crash. Final Destination 2 is sometimes more serious, sometimes lighter, introduces new characters and makes Ali Larter secondary. Devon Sawa is nowhere to be found. Tony Todd makes scary faces and says scary things again. Horror fans will geek on it as much as the mainstream audience.

We're here for the imaginative kills and we get a lot of it. It isn't as eerie and mysterious as the original, but it spares us a redundant procedural. It trades scares for action and vulnerability for resilience. By tradition, it starts with carnage and ends with carnage. In the middle is nothing but immature and stretched out suspenseful gore, courtesy of characters we don't really care about.

WILLARD
2003

7/8
A troubled man discovers he shares a psychic link with rats and uses them in a revenge plot.

This is the second screen adaptation of a novel by Stephen Gilbert. Every second of it is enchanting, thanks to a mystical trio composed of Crispin Glover, a creepy sociopath, his invasive and annoying mother, played by Jackie Burroughs, and R. Lee Ermey, a persecuting boss who's everything Willard despises and vice versa. All characters are polarized versions of who they were in the 1971 version.

Glover owns every scene he's in and is particularly good when he's alone or spending time with rats. He also has strong one on one arguments with R. Lee Ermey's character, who nobody should bother debating with. The film is not technically a comedy, but it has a sharp sense of humor. We're the only ones laughing, mind you, this is otherwise a dark experience.

The way Willard gains influence among rodents is presented interestingly. We get a nice montage that makes us buy what the script is selling, including a supernatural element we never really question that lasts until the very end of the film. With its mesmerizing score and its superior directing, Willard is a unique horror movie you'll want to put at the top of your watch list.

DEAD END
2003

7/8

On Christmas Eve, on their way to a celebration, a family tries a shortcut and soon regrets it.

Dead End is as amusing as it is sinister. It's a Christmas-themed horror movie, but it couldn't be further from a celebration. It sends shivers down our spine on many occasions. It is suspenseful, it is sad, and it contains imaginative gore. The screenplay is clever and colorful. The film is told like a classic campfire tale. The budget is relatively small but that's never a problem.

Lin Shaye plays a mother who is losing grip on her family and, soon, on reality. Ray Wise is the abrupt and impatient husband and father, Mick Cain is the comic relief, Alexandra Holden the traumatized daughter and William Rosenfeld her boring boyfriend. These guys have great chemistry. We totally buy them as a family. When shit hits the fan, we sympathize instantly.

Most of the running time is spent inside and around a car, at night, and this probably wasn't easy to shoot. This movie being dialogue-driven, we're in good hands with writers and directors Jean-Baptiste Andrea and Fabrice Canepa. The actors deliver their lines effortlessly. It rolls off their tongues. The creators truly caught lightning in a bottle with Dead End.

IDENTITY
2003

7/8

Stranded at a desolate motel during a rain-storm, a group of strangers start dying one by one.

Two things make Identity a marvel. First, it has one of the best twists in film history. You won't see it coming. Second, it has an incredible ensemble cast. We're talking John Cusack, Ray Liotta, Amanda Peet, John Hawkes, Alfred Molina, Clea DuVall, Jake Busey and Rebecca De Mornay. How can you go wrong with a team like that? How is this casting even possible?

The film is very dynamic, unpredictable, sporadically gory, tense, scary and a little bit sad. We go through a wide range of emotions in a short period of time. In a nutshell, it is inspired by Ten Little Indians. You can say this, of course, of every whodunit, but it's especially true here. Identity has a surreal aspect to it, and it doesn't exclude the possibility of a supernatural element.

Trying to guess who the killer is can be frustrating. The creators just won't give that away easily. Have fun guessing, but you'll probably fail. There are so many layers to Identity that it's worth watching over and over. Several clues are dropped and you'll probably miss them all. This is, simply put, one of the best psychological thrillers of its decade.

BEYOND RE-ANIMATOR
2003

6/8

A scientist who discovered how to reanimate the dead is sent to prison where he resumes his experiments.

Herbert West's acolyte from the two previous movies is not returning. Another smart and vulnerable protagonist is introduced and he does an okay job at filling the void. It marks the end of a classic mad scientist duo but establishes a similar relationship. Dr. Carl Hill is not making an appearance either, but is matched by the twisted warden's eccentric persona and sick mind.

Beyond Re-Animator is both gory and funny. The actors do an excellent job. The cinematography is arguably the best it's been and the production doesn't look cheap, adjusting well to digital. The writing is up to par and the film never gets boring. There is always something gruesome being talked about, eluded to or fully shown, and always with tongue in cheek in an attempt to uphold the tradition.

The script makes the global storyline progress rather than remake itself. After all, the source material has such great potential. It still treats its main protagonists as good guys, though West is rightfully sentenced to death and therefore confined for the whole running time. We manage to forgive him for his evil acts, disregarding his murder rate simply because his character is so hilarious.

BEST HORROR MOVIES OF 2004

SAW
2004

8/8

Chained to pipes in a disused bathroom, two men are given a puzzle to which they must provide answers.

Saw is both a torture film and a police procedural. It's a ongoing mystery that explores new grounds in storytelling. It's refreshing and unique, yet closely reminiscent of the Cube franchise and Se7en. The power of this movie resides in how it cleverly parses clues, how complex the puzzle is, and how twists and turns reveal themselves. They do so in the most creatively shocking fashion.

The writing is brilliant. The photography is impeccable. Extreme color balance, photo filters and quick editing gives this movie a particular trademark. The actors do a fine job of keeping us guessing, sympathizing, cringing. Their performances make you feel as powerless as their characters become. One of the two main plot lines happens in one place and with only two characters.

While the cast is limited, each of their movements, lines and performances has been scrutinized and polished. When dialogue makes room for gore, Saw shows another significant strength; displaying pain and suffering crudely and realistically, thanks to stunning top-of-the line effects. Innovative, yet formulaic, Saw gives us a new horror icon with its own sonata; a nod to slasher flicks.

THE BUTTERFLY EFFECT
2004

7/8

A man afflicted by a supernatural disease learns to travel back in the past to make the present better.

The Butterfly Effect is a tragic supernatural thriller that deals with time travel in its own creative way using a logic we haven't seen before. Its main protagonist, Ashton Kutcher's character, uses passages from private journals he wrote to revisit his youth and alter the past to make the present better; better for him, his friend and his love interest.

The film deals with difficult subjects like pedophilia, violence, bad parenting, mental illness, physical disability, suffering and death. It is a story about regrets and remorse, of things we would've done differently had we known the consequences of our acts. Despite and implausible plot, this movie is extremely sad, very serious and highly introspective.

And, aside its complex concept, the script doesn't have major plot holes. For such a tragic story, it even has its fun moments. The writing is fine, the directing irreproachable, and the actors are so good they make us forget we're watching fiction. This movie passes by so fast it leaves us wanting more. The gimmick is poignant and strangely addicting.

#3

CLUB DREAD
2004

7/8

A serial killer is stalking and murdering the employees and guests of a paradise island.

Coconut Pete's Coconut Beach Resort is the best place on Earth and the Broken Lizard collective is about to prove it. This may very well be the best movie they made, and it's a slasher slapstick comedy, of all things. This film is guaranteed to put a smile on your face. It contains a ridiculous number of red herrings, alcohol, drugs, and sex at every turn.

Many filmmakers attempted to make parodies of horror movies, but few succeeded the way Club Dread does. In most cases, they didn't care enough about character exposition, which is prominent, here. Club Dread was written by Jay Chandrasekhar, Kevin Heffernan, Steve Lemme, Paul Soter and Erik Stolhanske, who all play important characters. These guys are the bee's knees.

The men and woman, in this, aren't wearing much. Women are particularly beautiful. The casting is lightning in a bottle. This is, in a nutshell, one of the most feel-good horror comedy out there, with emphasis on "comedy". There are plot holes throughout, yes, but that comes with the territory. This film makes absolutely no sense and it's perfect this way. Blame it on surrealism.

DAWN OF THE DEAD
2004

7/8
Strangers take refuge in a mall during a zombie outbreak.

Those coming into this unaware of the classic horror movie it remakes will have their mind blown and will fully appreciate the ride regardless. This film stands alone but honors a great legacy. Hardcore fans of George A. Romero's work will recognize antisocial patterns of 1985's dramatic Day of the Dead transported in shopping mall sets reminiscent of 1978's more comedic Dawn of the Dead.

The zombies look amazing, but they run and twitch. Because our leads must survive a while for a movie to exist, the living dead are limited in number to compensate for their speed and strength. The only issue this creates, here, is that the mall isn't invaded, per say, until late in the story. It feels like a wasted gimmick at first, but the script wants to depict human conflicts instead.

Writer James Gunn is familiar with Romero's ways. He purposely isolates the victims; a powerful ensemble cast of popular names, from the zombies for most of the runtime to force them to survive creatively, in addition to dealing with the alienation, the infection, the claustrophobia and the paranoia. He knows that the living dead are simple villains that generate rhetorical story arcs.

CUBE ZERO
2004

7/8
A prison operator infiltrates the rigged labyrinth he controls to save a victim.

The little backstory and the few answers Cube 2: Hypercube provided led us to believe humans; possibly government officers, were nothing more than suited scientists of the future doing cervical experiments. Some might have felt Part 2 revealed too much and undershot the enigma. Cube: Zero, presumably a prequel, takes place in the rusty rooms and around the traps of a three-dimensional prototype.

What's more, evil is given at least four faces. Two of them are compelling protagonists who set a fun tongue-in-cheek tone. They are the better part of the backstory we get; other bits going as far as imaging life outside the cube that should have ended up on the cutting room floor. We are fed too much detail about the fact this this one takes place in the future and in our world.

We care little for the people inside the maze since we already know how their story goes and ends. Zachary Bennett plays Eric, the most interesting and strongest character in the franchise. He is who we worry about. His arc is immense and his perspective on the mystery makes him the perfect protagonist of a smart, well-written sequel. Part 1 was great, Part 2 was good and Part 0 is a blast!

BEST HORROR MOVIES OF 2005

HOUSE OF WAX
2005

7/8

A group of teens stranded in a village near a strange wax museum realize their lives are in danger.

Elisha Cuthbert, Jared Padalecki, Paris Hilton, and Chad Michael Murray make this film epic, though it would still impress without them. They're not just talented actors, they remind us of people we know. They make this film fun and comfortable before it gets increasingly dark. This is the second time this story gets remade, and it is quite an enhancement. It's a slasher with an edge.

The writers know what a good movie is and that's exactly what they're giving us. They bank on common horror tropes, half the time, and somewhat re-invent them otherwise. The antagonists follow the same logic. We've seen their patterns before, but never quite like this. The budget is substantial, and the movie needs it to tell a big story. The set decoration and the special effects are massive.

Some of the pain inflicted is atrocious and, at times, hard to watch. The gore is brilliant. In regard to who bites the dust and in which order, the script does a pretty good job of keeping us guessing and on the edge of our seat. Personality flaws end up being assets. People we thought were protected by the writers get mutilated. You just can't take anything for granted. Great flick!

SAW II
2005

7/8

A SWAT team leader negotiates with a terminally ill murderer in attempt to save his son from a poison and a booby-trapped maze.

Jigsaw, the contraption serial killer, gathered a bunch of people in a condemned building and puts them to the test, again; this time as a group. Pushed to their limits, all characters eventually become hostile to each other. This is, in a way, Saw on a larger scale. The pace is faster, the cast larger, and the game more complex.

The story blends well with the first movie, some characters return and there is stunning continuity. The visual style and the filtered photo match the original picture. No plot detail is left to chance and every subplot finds its purpose. Expect the same score, excellent performances, significant production quality, the same frantic editing, and, of course, high shock and stress value.

Half of it takes place in Jigsaw's workshop, with a villain on the verge of death and with nothing to lose: someone that can't be threatened or reasoned with. He watches people die one by one in the most creative ways, something we now expect from the creators. The gimmick is simple: suffer or die suffering. It's not much of a choice, but it's terrifyingly relatable and horribly satisfying...

THE JACKET
2005

7/8

A war veteran is sent to a mental institution where he becomes the object of a doctor's experiments allowing him to revisit the past.

The Jacket features an amazing cast of widely acclaimed stars, big and small at the time. We're talking Adrien Brody, Keira Knightley, Jennifer Jason Leigh, Daniel Craig, and Kris Kristofferson. Imagine The Butterfly Effect, but darker. Yes, darker. One Flew Over the Cuckoo's Nest's is vanilla compared to this. We're dealing with time travel, on the fringe of mental illness.

Brody doesn't own a time traveling DeLorean, but he spends most of his time in a morgue drawer, restrained by a straitjacket, something Doctor Kristofferson is fond of. He then revisits the past and tries to fix a few things. Way to mix horror and time travel! This film grabs you by the crotch and never lets go. It keeps you guessing, and it probably won't end well.

When stellar writing, directing, and editing come together, no matter how complex your story is, you're bound to leave a mark, impress, and become a reference. The stars aligned for this film to succeed. Terror and sadness are a deadly mix. They make great horror films if they hit the right notes. Let's face it; psychosis is next to godliness in fiction, and this film banks on it.

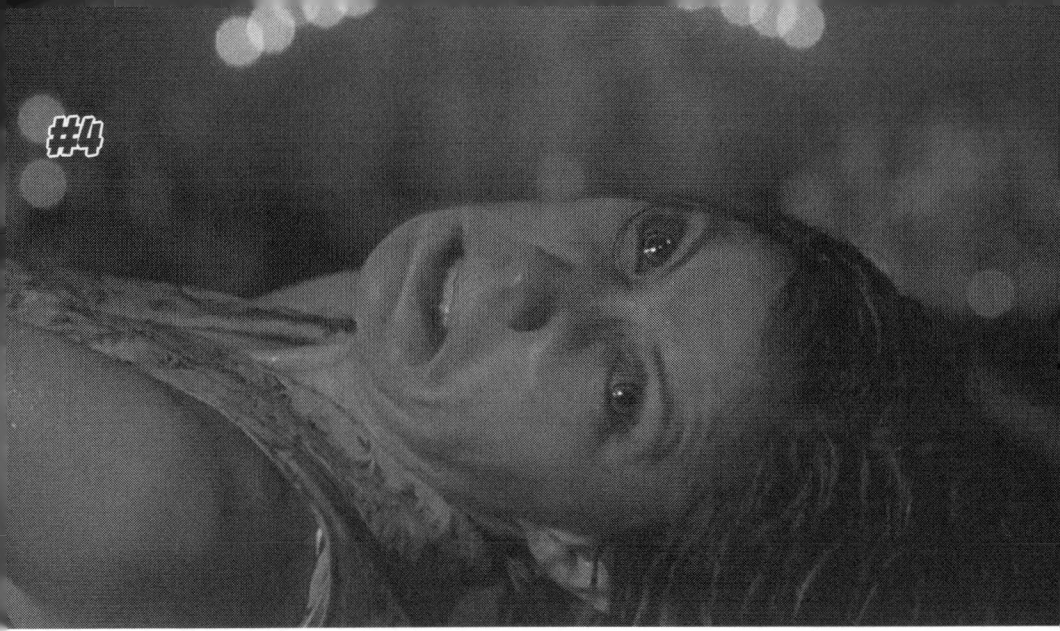

THE EXORCISM OF EMILY ROSE
2005

7/8

A lawyer takes on a homicide case involving a priest who performed an exorcism on a girl.

1973's The Exorcist set the bar pretty high in terms of possession movies. Perhaps the goal was never to beat the classic, but, rather, to address exorcism differently. The Exorcism of Emily Rose is a trial film and a legal procedural with a strong religious layer. These subgenres don't often collide and the end result, in this case, is enthralling.

This film reaches its full potential on several occasions, when the calm and the slow pacing of the procedural are sporadically interrupted by loud and frightening sequences of possession. We're constantly caught off-guard. So, is Emily epileptic, psychotic or downright possessed? You'll find out soon enough. Emily's hallucinations are terrifying, and her contortions are petrifying.

Although all actors do a bang-up job, Jennifer Carpenter is killing it. While this story isn't all about her, and despite the fact that her scenes are in fact flashbacks, she's the center of attention. The writers feel they need to punctuate Laura Linney's character's life with demonic manifestations, and those sometimes feel forced, often meeting a dead end. It is the script's only major flaw.

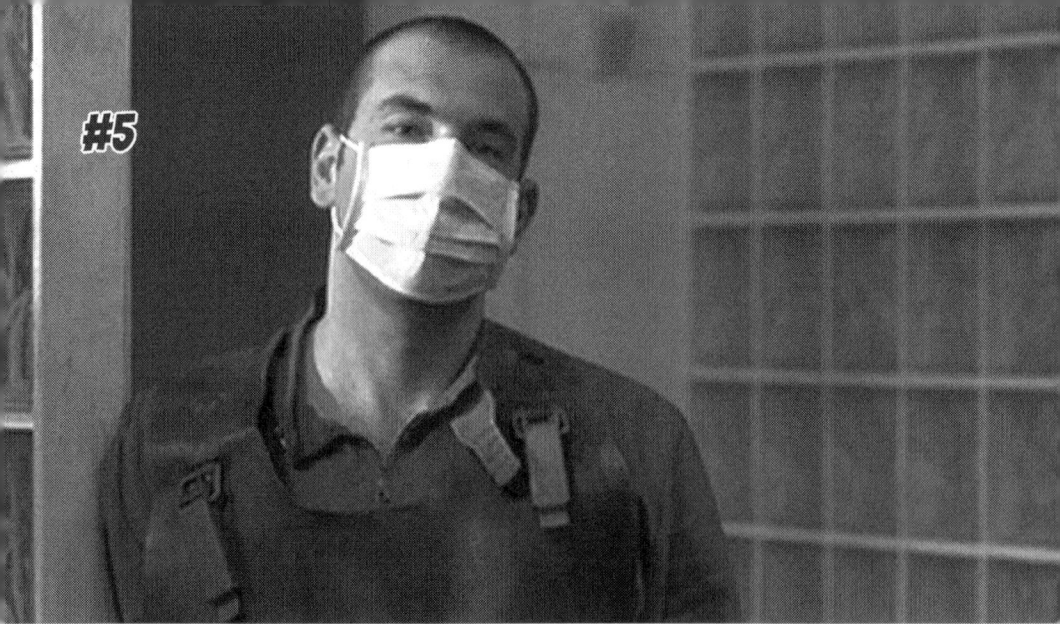

HOSTEL
2005

7/8

Three friends travel to Slovakia to party and have sex but find danger instead.

On the surface, Hostel is a thriller about friends backpacking far, in a distant region, where they eventually get in big trouble. A good amount of time is spent exposing the main characters, making them people we'd love to know and would rather not see suffer when the main threat hits them. This film contains exhaustive character exposition, but gory torture is its main attraction.

You can call Hostel misogynist and xenophobic; the truth is it strikes where it hurts and it's usually what horror movies strive to do. It's highly exploitative, it's scary, and it's supported by great sets that sometimes inspire freedom, sometimes terror. It plays on our fear of the unknown but by stripping away all potential surrealism and keeping it real. This is as visceral as horror gets...

The film piggy backs on our fear of racism, terrorism and wars. The special effects are built to make the audience cringe and, to that effect, near perfection. Even considering many small parts necessitated the local casting of actors who can't speak English, the dialogue generally comes out as authentic. Hostel will shock many but, in the end, deserves to be called a classic.

BEST HORROR MOVIES OF 2006

FINAL DESTINATION 3
2006

7/8

Teenagers saved from a roller coaster incident by a psychic friend are stalked and killed by Death.

The tragic and over the top intro mayhem, here, takes place in a theme park and sets the tone for a carnivalesque sequel. The writers are getting more superficial, the effects more ambitious; though not always convincingly polished, and the actors are effervescent. The cast was renewed again, for better or worse, and assigned paper thin personas hard to bond with.

It's a little sexier, much dumber, immature, and it bends the gimmick's rules. Somewhat a copy/paste of the original film, Final Destination 3 eventually meets a dead end. Since Tony Todd, the only face we can attribute to the Reaper, isn't showing up, any hope for backstory is loss. There is no mystery left to explore. Continuity is from now on hindered and any attempt at a procedural is futile.

The kills are getting creative and edited in a way to feel parodically stretched. The gore is extreme, imaginative, and feels earned because build-up is well paced. This is still a high budget production but one that takes many shortcuts. We're losing layers, actors, characters, locations, and our connection to the original story; therefore getting a simpler, quintessential slasher in return.

SAW III
2006

7/8

Threatened by a deadly contraption, a doctor must perform brain surgery on her dying captor.

Two stories are being told at once. We follow both a surgeon who's forced to save the villain's life and a man stuck in an improvised labyrinth whose backstory is unclear. By now, we know we're in for gore and crazy twists. The two previous narrative structures were more intricately crafted, but this is by no mean a weak sequel. It certainly doesn't hold back.

The film's biggest weakness is that it pushes the creativity so far that it loses the shocking plausibility of the previous films. We're increasingly asked to suspend disbelief. The writing is still smart; just not its usual self. The horror, in this franchise, has been emanating from a clever, horrifying mix of dilemmas and schemes set up by an evil genius. This element is stronger than ever.

The torture devices are more aesthetic; not the ones that necessarily rip you apart. The editing is sometimes abusive, but then it also keeps things quick, with minimal dialogue and little filler. Continuity is remarkable. Even when considering the artistic liberties taken, this one is as homogeneous as the first sequel was; so much so that the series is slowly starting to feel like one big movie.

PERFUME: THE STORY OF A MURDERER
2006

7/8

Born with a superior olfactory sense, a man attempts to create the world's finest perfume.

Perfume: The Story of a Murderer is a German period crime thriller. The screenplay is based on Patrick Süskind's 1985 novel Perfume about the sense of smell and its emotional impact. It is narrated, almost from beginning to end, by an unidentified voice. The film is so skillfully made that we can almost smell stench and the various perfumes presented to us.

As poetic and magical as Perfume is, it is, as the title indicates, the story of a serial killer. There are two dominant elements at play, here; Grenouille's supernatural power and his obsession for women. Dead women. In fact, he needs them dead to preserve their essence because there's no way they will cooperate through "enfleurage", his sinister extraction process.

The score is as ambitious as the photo and pretty much every aspect of this film. If you don't like Perfume, it just isn't for you. It's certainly not flawed. It is highly immersive and downright intoxicating; it's a trip inside the mind of a psychopath who we somehow relate to until we no longer can. The closer he gets to his goal, the more he loses our sympathy, until a memorable last act.

BEHIND THE MASK: THE RISE OF LESLIE VERNON
2006

6/8
Three filmmakers document a serial killer's routine.

When it comes to homages and parodies of slasher films, there is Scream and then there's Behind the Mask. The two brands are very entertaining and have nothing in common. The faux-documentary approach of Behind the Mask really grows on you. It's not what you would call a found footage movie, because, every so often, the creators use conventional film language to tell the story.

There are Easter eggs and cameos in the first act. The film mostly spoofs Halloween, Nightmare on Elm Street and Friday the 13th. It's fun to see the killer justify slasher tropes; stereotypes, body count, the obsession for virgins and final girls, doing a bad job of convincing us that this somehow makes sense. The filmmakers manage to keep us on the edge of our seat all along.

Behind the Mask doesn't just make fun of horror villains, it creates a new one. It's about the members of family who do not only kill but also learned to fake their death. Leslie Vernon always has a trick up his sleeve to escape death and lure his victims; sleigh of hands, illusion, scare tactics, and the list goes on. This is definitely one for the horror fans. This movie deserves a sequel!

THE BUTTERFLY EFFECT 2
2006

6/8

A man realizes he can travel back in time and alter the present by looking at pictures of himself.

The main protagonist, here, deserves a bit of his bad fortune. Contrary to Ashton Kutcher's character, in the first film, Eric Lively's character is superficial and uses his powers to achieve frivolous goals. His ambitions are mostly professional. He doesn't value life and can't appreciate his girlfriend. He isn't that likable and certainly not relatable, but his story is interesting nonetheless.

With this new installment, this emerging franchise ages surprisingly well. This sequel is both similar and different enough from the original that it is worth watching. It does't feel redundant and is supported by a decent script. It hits the same sad notes Part 1 did, though more moderately, and features convincing actors who match the collective talent the original cast had.

The Butterfly Effect 2 exploits themes such as friendship, love, money, the ego, adulthood, business, regrets, suffering and death. Perhaps the film doesn't use its gimmick as much as it should. It certainly doesn't use it as much as the original movie did. The hero uses his powers like they're a genie in a bottle instead of truly trying to fix the past to avoid collateral tragedies.

BEST HORROR MOVIES OF 2007

1408
2007

8/8
A man is trapped inside a hotel room and terrorized by ghosts.

At its purest form, 1408 is a condensed version of The Shining. This is obvious. The film is based on a short story by Stephen King and he can rip off his own material if he feels like it, but is it worth watching? 1408 needs to be considered a stand alone film and appreciated as such. It contains enough fresh material and twists you won't see coming. All in all, this is a great movie. Here's why...

First, it stars John Cusack in one of the best roles of his glorious career. Samuel L. Jackson is there to shuffle the deck. He wants to help, he's friendly, yet he's ominous. This is one of the most claustrophobic horror movies ever made. It's basically about a man stuck in a hotel room from another dimension. He should be surrounded by people and traffic, yet he couldn't be more isolated.

The acting is irreproachable. The limited set and cast are an advantage. Horror is mostly psychological, here, and it will send shivers down your spine on many occasions. One of 1408's creepiest cards is making your imagination wander. Exactly how far does room 1408's reach extends? At what point, in the film, does the haunting start? The more you think, the scarier this film gets...

TRICK 'R TREAT
2007

7/8

A Halloween night turns into a blood bath for different groups of people connected to each other.

This is one of the best horror anthology films ever made. It is right up there with Creepshow and Trilogy of Terror. It sets itself apart from the norm by the way it intertwines 6 segments. Things happen before, during and after another, and we're never sure in which order. The script is brilliantly layered in a way to juxtapose stories seamlessly. Michael Dougherty orchestrates this like a king.

The photography is so precise and so optimized that Dougherty earns our attention from frame one. The scary parts are scary, the build-up is outstanding, the gore striking, the stories original and the twists surprising. Gore feels real and so does the rest of the effects. Trick 'r Treat's major flaw is that its tales feel incomplete despite an intention to innovate with a new kind of narrative.

Story 1 doesn't stand on its own but sets the tone nicely. Story 2 is about a man who gives a kid poisoned candy. Story 3 follows a bunch of teenagers who play a prank on a friend. Story 4 is about a special party in a remote location. Story 5 introduces a small demonic character who will teach a hermit a lesson. This is the best story in the pack. Story 6 ties the last lose ends nicely.

DEATH PROOF
2007

7/8
An ex-stuntman stalks different groups of women.

This jewel is written and directed by Quentin Tarantino. It is arguably one of his best movies. The man's strength and trademark have always been and will probably always be his dialogue. His second defining characteristic is his irregular pacing. In Death Proof, he once again pulls the non-linear gimmick and stretches time, keeping little focus on actual horror.

Kurt Russel plays an extremely laid back and eccentric character who doesn't exactly look like a serial killer. His murder weapon is concealed until late in the story. He shares the screen with a bunch of sexy women who all sound like Tarantino when they express themselves. This is a bit creepy. Death Proof is split in two portions. The second portion is a re-imagining of the first one.

The movie pays homage to exploitation and muscle car films of the 1970s. Some shots are heavily edited and composited in a way to look like they were made in Technicolor, with deep blacks, bright whites and a decoloration. The actors all give superior performances and feel at ease with dialogue that is everything but easy to work with. Tarantino gets his unique vision across, as always.

THE MIST

2007

7/8

A mist unleashes bloodthirsty creatures on a small town, where a band of citizens hole up in a supermarket.

Frank Darabont, director and screenwriter, proves once again that he can adapt Stephen King's material like no one else. He can deliver, within budget, a stunning production quality. The actors are solid. The casting is excellent. Everybody fits their part. The action mainly takes place in one location; a grocery store, and the film is apparently shot on a sound stage. It's so claustrophobic!

The screenplay is ambitious. The creature design and most of the storyline could be described as Lovecraftian. The creatures' origin is and will remain a mystery. Their goal and motivations are never explained. As one of the character suggests, at some point, they are either supernatural, biblical or man-made. They could be anything. It's what makes them creepy. The mist itself is an enigma.

The 3D effects are a little too shiny for my taste, and that's the film's only flaw. As is often the case in apocalyptic movies, human's most resilient enemies are other humans. Religion and spirituality are crucial to the plot. Romance and family are important themes, too. The Mist is frightening, introspective, but it's also terribly sad. And what a great ending!

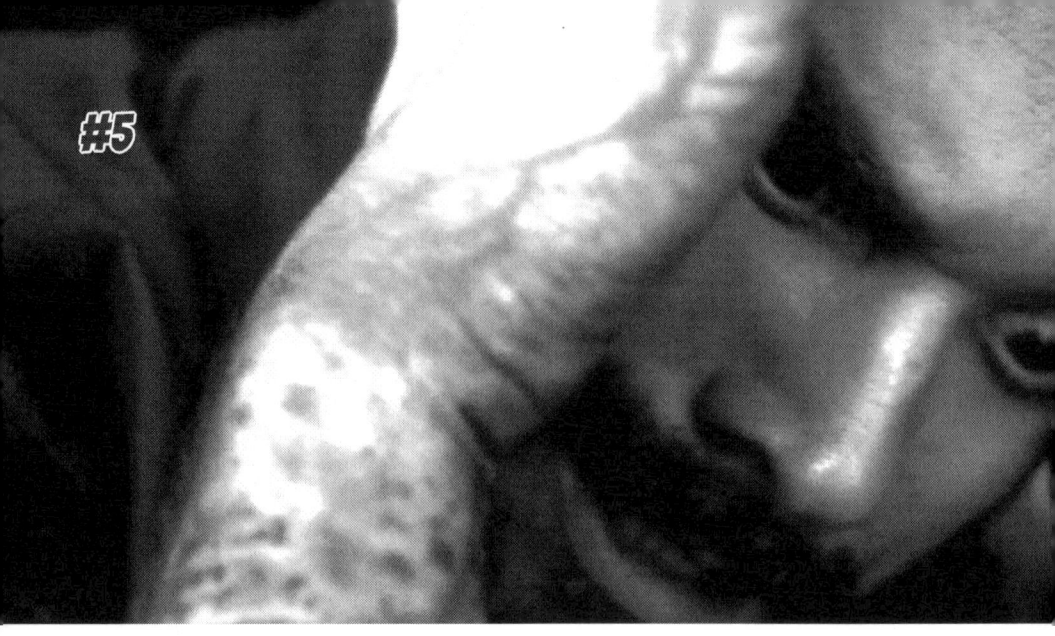

THE SIGNAL
2007

7/8

A mysterious electronic transmission turns people into killers.

The Signal is told in three parts with a non-linear structure; each written and directed by their own filmmaker. The segments all blend together seamlessly. This apocalyptic scenario is, ironically, much more plausible yet imaginative than a zombie outbreak, presented as it is. We're talking contagious psychosis and mass hysteria caused by static frequencies.

This mindfuck will take you to such extremities that you might end up laughing and shivering at the same time. It is so sensational that it will probably stick with you long after it's over. It is melancholic, sick and twisted, and then some. The humor is on and off, and it acts as an accelerant to the shock factor. The film is extremely gory and no character gets spared when it comes to violence.

The middle segment is the most interesting one. It uses creative ways to take actors in and out of the frame to interchange them, and therefore to simulate everyone's hallucinations. We can't tell if special effects or compositing are involved, or if the actors and the camera are perfectly synchronized instead, but we know this isn't a big budget production and we never question what we see.

BEST HORROR MOVIES OF 2008

PONTYPOOL
2008

7/8

A radio host interprets the possible outbreak of a deadly virus contracted vocally.

Radio stations are such an atmospheric place to set horror movies. They're isolated, small spaces, and they require a limited cast. Radio hosts are often the first to learn about disasters and other incidents, and they warn the population about potential danger. Radio stations, ironically, are not protected from invasions by zombies and other contagious creatures.

We've got three talented leads. Stephen McHattie gives the most memorable performance as the news anchor. He has a witty sense of humor and gets the best lines. He's a little eccentric and somewhat self-centered. The relationship between him and his colleagues is particular. There's his ex and his assistant. We instantly buy their unusual chemistry.

The dialogue gets increasingly hypnotic, as the story unfolds. We're dealing with a disease that spreads vocally. That concept, in itself, is extremely imaginative. The fact that we absorb most of the explanation shows proficient writing. Our mind is constantly fucked with, but we always have an understanding of what the characters are going through. Lightning in a bottle!

AMUSEMENT
2008

6/8
Three women share a dark fate.

Amusement is one of the best horror anthology movies to feature plausible content exclusively. The wrap around story is smart. It blends gradually and seamlessly. A few screenwriters have attempted this in recent years but rarely with so much tact and such good pacing. Amusement was directed by someone who definitely knows what he's doing and was written just as brilliantly.

There are three segments, here. The first is about a couple on a road trip who accept to travel in a convoy and soon regret their choice. The second is about a babysitter who is terrorized by a human-size clown doll that may be alive. The last one tells the story of a couple who go looking for their missing friend inside a hotel whose owner they find suspicious.

The killer, AKA "The Laugh", is played by an unrecognizable Keir O'Donnell, who proved to be a true chameleon. He is unidentifiable, even in plain sight. He sometimes wears prosthetics or is otherwise filmed in a way to partially conceal his face. This is a visual challenge whose success is hard to predict on paper, so the film deserves to be praised for it.

REPO! THE GENETIC OPERA
2008

6/8
A biotech company launches an organ-financing program.

Darren Lynn Bousam directs this little gem right in the midst of working on Saw 2, 3 and 4, and this influence can be seen all over. Repo! The Genetic Opera has a fascinating visual signature; a combination of gaussian blur and color filters. It is heavily digitally processed in post-production. The character design is astonishing and the set design simply breath-taking.

The transitions between key scenes is marked by comic book illustrations that keep us up to date on the storyline, because, let's face it, the songs themselves aren't enough. And that's the problem with this musical... the songs aren't very good or profound and they don't help the story progress. The singers aren't always on the note and some can barely sing. There's more rapping than singing, here.

Repo! eroticizes surgery and medical play in general. In a twisted way, this movie is kinky as hell. While almost no songs can be called earworms, look out for two exceptions: "At the Opera Tonight" and "Zydrate Anatomy". Ultimately, if the film's songs were all just as good, we might have a perfect picture. Seriously, what's a musical with bad song worth?

HELLBOY II: THE GOLDEN ARMY

2008

6/8

A demon and his team must save the world from mythical creatures.

This is a fantastic film. It builds on the structure established by its predecessor, the original Hellboy, and brings back several characters, big and small. It introduces an interesting array of villains, and it makes some of the old protagonists more prominent. It even adds to the origin story, but it doesn't really linger on the past. It takes for granted that we know Hellboy by now.

If Hellboy wasn't so arrogant, we wouldn't have this sequel. This storyline depicts him as a show-off who can't stay in the shadows. Can the boy from hell really be Earth's saviour? One thing's certain, he should start worrying about the new villains. They look badass. The set design, too, is something else. The architecture is breath-taking and right out of a role-playing game.

Hellboy 2 happens neither in the past, nor the future. It's action, adventure, science fiction, horror, and fantasy. It borrows from various genres and subgenres, at different times, but it's its own world, a world imagined by comic book artist Mike Mignola, and writer/director Guillermo del Toro. It's not for everyone, but those it's for will absolutely love it.

SAW V
2008

6/8

The survivor of a decimated cult forces a dangerous puzzle upon a handful of people, including a special agent that is tailing him.

The fifth installment in the Saw franchise spends time with serial killer Jigsaw's widow as she receives her mysterious inheritance. On the other hand, we get to know our newly established antagonist who carries the game master's legacy and we're not exactly sure why. The script simply doesn't offer plausible incentives. Somewhere in the middle of this, a group of people must cooperate to survive.

What used to be an ideology slowly turns into the elaborate criminal schemes of a corrupted cop. While we are far from the simplified complexity of 2004's Saw, we're given a refreshing game of dogs, cats and mice that the writers manage to keep interesting from beginning to end. This feels like a transitional sequel that ends where the last one stopped and sets the table for another installment.

Consequently, Saw V is hard to synopsize and appreciate on its own. It does live up to expectations, though, in regards to acting, writing and directing. You'll get what you expect, gore and creative torture devices included, but you might want to be up-to-date with the franchise before giving it a try. It is indissociable from its predecessors but pulls enough fresh intrigues to please the fan.

BEST HORROR MOVIES OF 2009

DRAG ME TO HELL
2009

7/8
A loan officer becomes the recipient of a supernatural curse.

When it comes to horror movies, Sam Raimi knows more than you do what's good for you. He pulls many tricks that he experimented with in the Evil Dead franchise. That is where he learned to build tension, make us laugh and frighten us, sometimes all at once. This is a very stressful film with excellent build-up, well-written characters and incessant terror.

The film is naturally paced, yet extremely calculated. When you're not scared, you're disgusted or feel terrible for Alison Lohman's adorable character. Witchcraft is a recurring theme. There is gore at every corner. The effects are 90% amazing and 10% made of bad CG. Who cares; this is one fun roller coaster ride that will make you laugh and jump just as much.

The jump scares are earned. The actors are irreproachable. The slapstick comedy gives Drag Me to Hell its signature. It wouldn't be half as interesting without it. Prepare to meet one of the most despicable and repulsive horror villains ever imagined. Sure, the story is kind of hard to keep up with and the ending is kind of weak, but most of this film is an absolute blast.

CABIN FEVER 2: SPRING FEVER
2009

7/8

A bottling factory unknowingly supplies a batch of contaminated water to a high school before prom night.

A frame-by-frame 2-D cartoon zip us through miles of unnecessary explanations, during the introduction credits, in regards to the plague's prolificity. No longer confined to a specific area, it spreads to the city; a high school, in this case, right before prom. Although some students are relatable, you can't worry about anyone's death, here. They all seem well-aware of their own tragic destiny.

Cabin Fever had humans as threat, and this was probably too much in the same film. The main gimmick is strong enough and this sequel knows it. It learns from the unmarketable aspects of the original and offers us a mainstream story that doesn't feel like every other one. It is cheesy, disgusting, but the story unveils more naturally because it embraces comedy.

Between the blood, pus, sperm and vomit hides tender tongue-in-cheek romance and easy satire. It's a smart movie purposely dumbed down and tinkered with in post-production but not for a dumb audience. It's namely an homage to prom night themed horror films of the 70's and 80's but delivered as a contamination flick. Entertaining from beginning to end, this is a no-brainer but a must-see!

ORPHAN
2009

7/8

A couple who recently lost their baby adopt a girl who is not nearly as innocent as she appears to be.

When it comes to evil kid movies, Orphan is as good as it gets. Half of those are repetitive, formulaic, poorly paced, and predictable. Orphan avoids every pitfall imaginable, walking on eggs, fully aware of how tricky this subgenre is. Half of evil kids' movies have a supernatural premise. Orphan doesn't, but it has a strong aura of mystery. It's very suspenseful, too.

Isabelle Fuhrman plays the adopted child referred to in the title. There's something wrong with her from the get-go. Her clothes are from another era, and she has a menacing vibe. Nothing good can come of her and Vera Farmiga's character, her new mom, soon regrets sheltering her. Peter Sarsgaard, the husband, is not a bad actor, but he lives in Farmiga's shadow.

Calling Farmiga mesmerizing would be an understatement. She tends to pick great scripts, and I can't think of a bad film she's been in. Her performance is stellar. That said, Fhurman is the pièce de résistance, here. Her part is pivotal. She's an amazing actress, and her character's arc is colossal. The third act of Orphan will send shivers down your spine. I guarantee it.

JENNIFER'S BODY
2009

7/8
A possessed high school cheerleader turns into a succubus.

This movie falsely attempts to glorify Megan Fox's beauty. In fact, as it turns out, Amanda Seyfried outcutes her. She has more depth, she's the girl next door, and, despite the film's title, this is her movie, not Fox's. The girls share a powerful bond. Lesbianism is addressed, but that's not where the focus is. In Jennifer's Body, Fox's character dies and comes back as a succubus.

What makes the picture so exciting is that the exposition happens before and after the inciting incident. When we're not watching a band play in a bar, we're spending time at school, at a dance or in suburbia. The creators really went for a cheerful vibe and familiar circumstances. The story is somewhat anachronic. If at first the plot seems illogical, know that it will eventually add up.

The acting is stellar. The characters completely immerse us. The soundtrack is fun. It's pretty much one song and it's made fun of repeatedly. If Seyfried's character wasn't so cynical, this movie would be at times touching. She ruins any attempt at romance. The film is scary, sexy, but also extremely funny when it turns into a comedy. Jennifer's Body is time well spent. It needs to be seen.

THE HUMAN CENTIPEDE (FIRST SEQUENCE)

2009

7/8

A mad doctor kidnaps and stitches together three tourists from anus to mouth.

There are few things worse than a car breakdown leading you under a psychopath's scalpel blade. Getting stitched buttock to mouth to your best friend and to a stranger by the hand of a mad surgeon is one of them. Rarely has torture porn used such a strong gimmick. The synopsis alone inspires fear and disgust. The Human Centipede is downright traumatizing and may make you sick.

Aside from some frustratingly improbable subplots, and despite the surreal premise, you buy what you see on screen. It's well shot and not as cheesy as one might think. There is pretty much a single location and a small amount of well fleshed characters. This setup allows for confined build-up that culminates into an amazing claustrophobic carnage so intense some might feel like pausing the film.

You will not want to eat before, during or after watching, and it will mark you for weeks. The disgusting stuff is mostly implicit and the gore limited, yet we feel the pain. It builds tension masterfully, makes you fear the worst, gives you even worse than implied, mixes humiliation, kink, sadism, fetishism, even. It's one sick movie, but it hits all the notes the ideal horror movie should.

BEST HORROR MOVIES OF 2010

SAW 3D: THE FINAL CHAPTER

2010

7/8

The members of a dangerous cult turn against each other as they reach the last steps of their master plan.

We start with another clever contraption and this one is displayed on the public place, curiously. The tone is momentarily that of a cheap slasher, and then we're back to a more familiar tone. Hoffman, the bad guy, survived the last film and is now angrier than ever. He made mistakes, recently, and attempts to clean up any trace of the past leading back to him. It's starting to feel like the end.

Some survivor we don't remember is put through a new series of traps but only delays the last call. It's the feud between Jigsaw's widow and his disciple we care about and we do get closure. The tension is palpable, as always, and we even manage to sympathize for the villain who's always so purposely deliciously underplayed. The other actors do an excellent job and are an interesting bunch.

This is also a reunion of everybody not yet dead; from previous movies or by implication. This brilliant subplot sets the perfect context for a meaningful massacre. Well directed, written and shot, and when considering how many loose ends need tying, the seventh installment in the Saw franchise pulls miracles, with twists at every turn. Here's a great conclusion to a great horror epic!

127 HOURS
2010

7/8

A mountain climber becomes trapped under a boulder while exploring canyons alone.

This film is based on Aron Ralston's memoir Between a Rock and a Hard Place. Aron is played by James Franco. This could be called the performance of a lifetime, but that's all the man ever does. His character meets a virtually unsolvable problem that threatens his life, and we witness his delirium and desperation as the story progresses. Franco makes us cherish our lives, however miserable.

127 hours is about a young man with his arm stuck between a boulder and a wall. The question is: is this story sustainable as a feature film? Is there enough meat on this bone? Surprisingly, yes. After a short introduction, the inciting event traps the protagonist. His only escapes, until the end, are his memories, flashbacks and hallucinations. The film otherwise takes place in one location.

The editing is cool, extreme and imaginative. It's there to speed up things, transmit the weather or to convey emotions; mostly regrets. The protagonist comes up with many ways to solve his problem and must deal with a great amount of frustration when they fail. This film is also a confession; the admission of an overgrown ego and excessive self-confidence. 127 Hours is a brutal therapy.

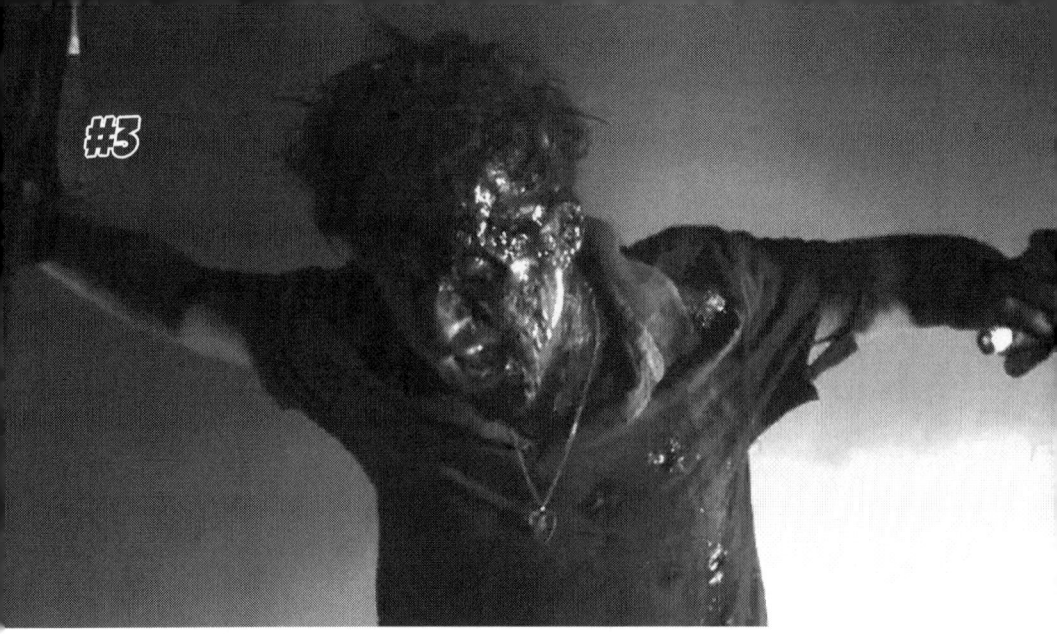

TUCKER AND DALE VS EVIL

2010

7/8

Two hillbillies on vacation at their mountain cabin get into a conflict with a group of college students.

Tucker and Dale vs Evil takes for granted that the audience know their scary movies and makes fun of the hillbilly horror subgenre in addition to the college student stereotype. A series of misunderstandings makes the college students presume that Tucker and Dale are evil, and, in return, they strike back. This premise probably sounds chaotic, but it will make sense.

This is a slasher flick without a serial killer. Tucker and Dale are the protagonists and whoever dies, here, dies by accident or by mistake. These deaths are are bunch of gory guilty pleasures. The body count is significant. The film has virtually no slow moments and little to no moralizing attempts. It's a horror comedy that avoids the pitfalls of the genre.

As one of the "college kids" puts it, at some point in the plot, most conflicts in history could've been avoided with better communication. This pretty much sums up what goes on in Tucker and Dale vs Evil. It is hilarious, then, to see that no character learns from this quote. These characters are unredeemable. They're clichés and they're only here to meet their maker for our viewing pleasure.

INSIDIOUS
2010

6/8

A family attempts to save their child from evil spirits that inhabit their new house.

Here's a contemporary ghost tale that feels like every other haunting film, except that it does most things better. The scary moments are earned, well-paced and always effective. The Poltergeist and Amityville Horror franchises have covered this ground, already, but there is nothing wrong with an updated cliche when the production value is so high and the script so delightful.

The cast is remarkable. A lot of the build-up relies on reactions from the characters to supernatural manifestations and the actors are giving a genuine slightly surreal performance. Those jump scares sure creep up on you; catching you when you least expect them because you care so much about the story that you forget it actually wants you to shiver every now and then.

Insidious is a quintessential haunted house flick done right and with clever variants. It is also an aggregation of the best of the subgenres it borrows from, and it's done right. The last half introduces antagonists with bizarre designs and ideas that may or may not work for you. The editing is noticeably frantic and cool rather than slow and eerie, but most of its eccentricities are welcome.

FROZEN
2010

6/8

3 skiers stranded on a chairlift are forced to make life-or-death choices to save their lives.

Five minutes into this film, you're already in love with the three protagonists. They're sympathetic extroverts, and they feel like our best friends. Basically, they're a couple and a third wheel. The dialogue flows. The chemistry works. This is the kind of movie in which characters are confined to one location with a life-threatening situation they can't possibly overcome, or can they?

The situation intensifies until they have no other choice but to gamble, make a dangerous move and risk their lives in exchange for their freedom. They must suffer in order to avoid death. This is a tragic story that makes us feel helpless. No matter how many times you watch this movie, it never gets merrier. This is one of the best pictures of its kind.

Not to give anything away, but this story is perfect until the wolves come ruin it all. At that point, writer Adam Green cheats his way out of a powerful gimmick he cannot keep up with. This said, everything else about Frozen is simply amazing. It's touching, sad, suspenseful, hopeless, frightening; it's everything a dark thriller should be. This is one of Adam Green's best movies.

BEST HORROR MOVIES OF 2011

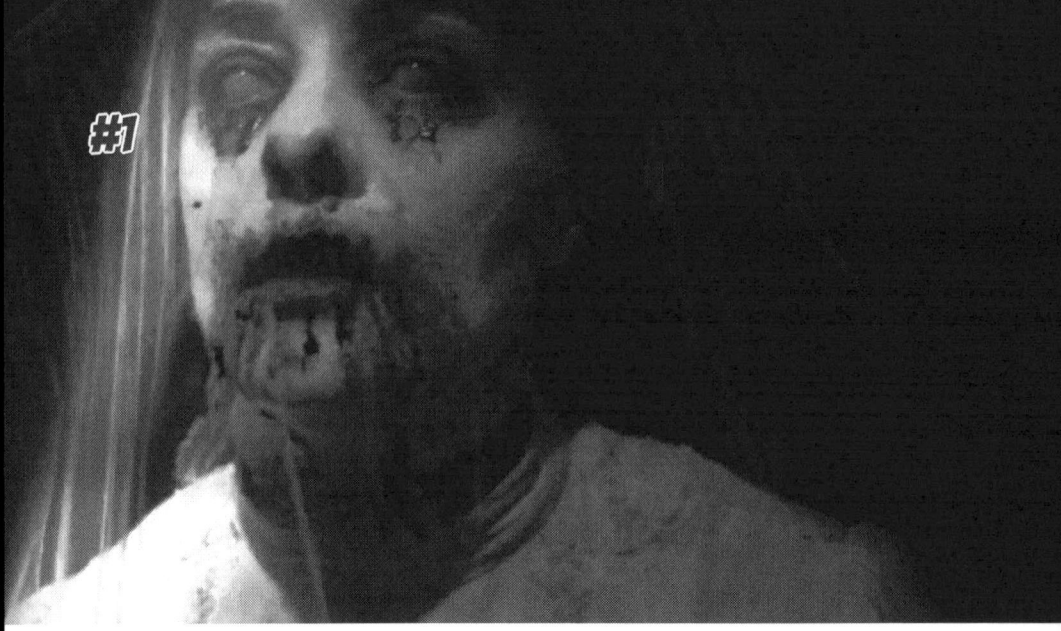

THE INNKEEPERS

2011

7/8

Two employees determined to reveal a hotel's haunted past experience disturbing events.

Watch the cutest, loveliest and most adorable pixie get bored for over 90 minutes when she should be seriously worried about her future. This is probably not going to end well for her. She is funny, fascinating and is extremely expressive, which allows her to carry most of the film on her shoulders. You'll hopefully fall in love with her. Ti West, writer and director, really wants you to.

There is wonderful chemistry between Sara Paxton and Pat Healy, which reflects on their respective characters. The strongest aspect of The Innkeepers is the exposition. The goal isn't as strong as the journey, so enjoy every second! This film was obviously inspired by Stanley Kubrick's The Shining. It is sprinkled with jump scares you won't soon forget.

Ti West's specialty is to let us simmer and never boil. Suspense in injected in small doses and the horror is close to inexistent, yet we expect it at every corner. Don't worry, by the time the end credit rolls, you'll be filled with terror and shivering. This is an unconventional ghost story and an excellent one. It is one of Ti West's best movies.

FINAL DESTINATION 5
2011

7/8

Survivors of a suspension-bridge collapse believe they are on Death's list.

Though it could be said all Final Destination films were great, true to their formula and clever with their self-writing gimmick, the franchise suffered a drop in plot quality as time passed. It had to purge itself two or three times from actors bigger than themselves who wouldn't return. The cast of Part 5 is once again reset, but not without purpose. The screenwriters work with and around it.

This is a rigorous production that learns from past mistakes. Part 3 & 4 were light in horror and poorly delivered. They somewhat took their audience for granted, dumbed down the global arc and hindered continuity. This one is more serious, more procedural, not as sensational at first glance but smartly written; as an apology for weaker entries and as a complement to the better ones.

You get one of the most grandiose introduction disasters yet, thorough character development, earned thrills and intense build-up rather than gore indulgence. Finally, prepare for what this series lacked most: answers and backstory. Final Destination 5 is as cohesive as Part 1 was, bigger on twist than any of its predecessors and a truly satisfying "conclusion"; a rare thing in horror franchises!

SCREAM 4

2011

7/8

While visiting her hometown during a book tour, the surviving victim of a series of massacres suspects she is the target of a new copycat killer.

The third Scream film was true to its formula but took the action to Hollywood, had a huge cast, and perhaps saw too big. Scream 4 brings us back to the simplicity of the original film. If Scream 2 was about sequels and Scream 3 about trilogies, this one is all about remakes. It is somewhat a revision of the first film; this time around, though, in a world of smart phones and webcams.

The series reboots itself by introducing an ensemble of young actors in a configuration similar to 1996's Scream's. They go to college and love horror movies, but grew up on movies like Scream and Saw; not Nightmare on Elm Street, Halloween and Friday the 13th. How's that for meta horror? Our three favorite leads return. The performers give it all they have and do a convincing job, as always.

It finds inspiration in an obvious era of remakes, found-footage horror and torture porn. The murders are rough and bloodier. The characters are varied but slightly underdeveloped. You wish you could spend quality time with them but the script is a little packed. Scream 4 plays it low key and feeds a certain nostalgia. It's yet another terrific sequel with excellent writing, directing and photo.

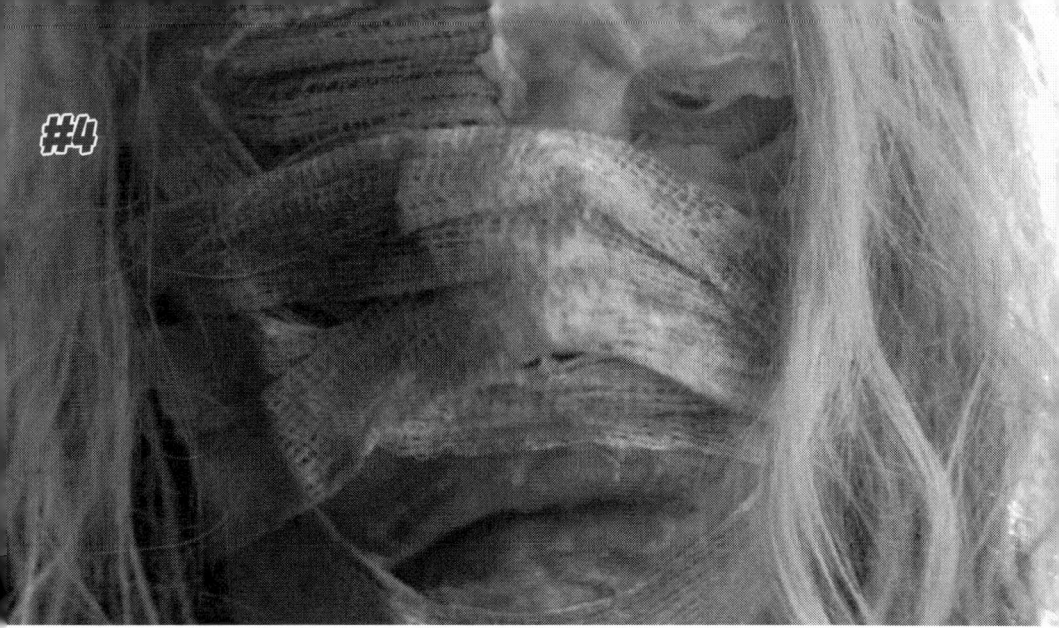

DETENTION
2011

7/8

A group of co-eds try to avoid being murdered by a serial killer while serving detention.

Detention has dense, hilarious integrated graphic design that might take a few revisits to fully grasp. The compositing, in fact, is one with the story. Characters interact with it, constantly breaking the fourth wall. The film is broken down into chapters, and the title cards can get confusing… somewhat pointless, at times. This movie is clever, but it's an acquired taste.

This is the millennial version of a slasher flick, except it's not exactly meant for them. Detention is a ninety-minute inside joke on the 1990's. 1992, if we want to get technical. It deals with time travel, and aliens, somehow. There's body horror, attempted suicide, a masked murderer. The film is all over the place. Humor-wise, it is the Napoleon Dynamite of horror movies.

Shanley Caswell is a solid protagonist, but Spencer Locke is the ultimate revelation. Though she first appears to be paper thin, her character ends up with the most interesting arc. Parker Bagley, the bully, will make you piss your pants. Detention contains one of the most creative and upbeat opening credits ever imagined in a horror movie, and what follows is absolutely fascinating.

THE HUMAN CENTIPEDE II (FULL SEQUENCE)

2011

7/8

A security guard obsessed by a horror movie attempts to recreate his favorite scenes by kidnapping people and stitching them together.

He's short, uncoordinated and doesn't speak. He's a psychopath and he's obsessed by the original Human Centipede movie. Meet Martin, a creepy security guard that brings you into his black and white world and into his progressive madness. We aren't following through with the first story, but actress Ashlynn Yennie returns as herself in a self-referential sequel that isn't short of surprises.

The ambiance is surreal, sweaty, and dirty. The most interesting aspect about the film is that Martin isn't a doctor, has a visibly low IQ, denies reality, and therefore neglects the complexity of surgery. The end result is gorier than the more implicit original. The protagonist and villain is a man-child surrounded by violence, abuse, and characters not much deeper than he is.

The Human Centipede franchise is one the mainstream audience knows about because of its evocative gimmick, but one that few dare watching; even hardcore horror fans. Both films seem to laugh at the viewers while challenging them not to look away. This one does it without the use of color, realistic dialogue and with a discomforting photography that makes us feel ill when exposed for too long.

BEST HORROR MOVIES OF 2012

PROMETHEUS
2012

7/8

A group of space archaeologists place their hopes on a star map said to lead to an ancient civilization.

It all confusingly starts with a translucent humanoid disintegrating, then the plot starts centering on a bored android who greets a group of people awakening from stasis aboard a spaceship. This addition in the Alien franchise tells the story of a scientific expedition motivated by existential hypotheses. The script is daring and shocks through unlikely devices; namely religions and beliefs.

An immersing exploration scene gradually pulls us from the sterility of the ship to the claustrophobic setting of an underground alien shrine. The environments are constantly evolving when not literally self-destructing for our enjoyment. This is a visually charged movie with a thin story and great performances. It also relies highly on dialogue and gets increasingly tense in the second act.

The creature effects, mostly practical, look amazing, eluding to the Aliens movies while teasingly remaining "everything but". The interior and exterior sets are once again a textured masterpiece. As a stand-alone film, this is the perfect excuse for a nice controversial blend of horror, adventure, science-fiction, science, faith and philosophy.

JOHN DIES AT THE END
2012

7/8
Two friends must save humanity from a new street drug that sends its users across time and dimensions.

So, the "Sauce", AKA "soy sauce", is a drug that turns people into psychics and brings back the dead, among other things, which means you're in for one hell of a ride. The humor is tongue-in-cheek and found at every turn. It's witty, sharp and you could even miss some jokes if you aren't fully paying attention. The writing and the execution are out of this world.

This is based on a book by the same title and brought to the screen by none other than Don Coscarelli, who gave us the Phantasm franchise. This film feels more intimate than his previous work. The dialogue is sometimes hilarious, sometimes profound and sometimes hypnotic. John Dies at the End is a legendary mindfuck. It is infinitely imaginative, and it is never boring.

Coscarelli makes every jump scare count. These aren't cheap scares. They're cleverly orchestrated and they're funny. Expect some penis jokes, along the way, impressive creature effects and hallucinations that will blow your mind. The "Sauce" is, in a nutshell, a drug with a direct link to hell. Its concept is unexpected, but its supernatural effects are strangely cohesive.

EXCISION

2012

7/8

A controlling mother drives her daughter insane.

Despite its surreal metaphors and its cynical attitude, Excision is a sad story; it's about the things that affect teenagers negatively, who then grow up to hate life and themselves. It's about bullying, disease; physical and mental, beliefs, parenting, beauty, or lack thereof, and violence. Pauline is a misfit but not necessarily an introvert. She's a go-getter, but in the creepiest ways.

She's played by the gorgeous AnnaLynne McCord. Richard Bates Jr., writer and director, basically took a hot chick and made her ugly to make a point. It doesn't matter how pretty you are when you have skeletons in your closet. She has shitty parents, she's unhinged, and she's dangerous. Her mother is Traci Lords, who plays the exact opposite of the person we know she is.

John Waters, Ray Wise, and Malcolm McDowell play school employees, adding a tongue-in-cheek layer to the equation. Excision is a comedy and a drama. It's an excellent movie. It's modern, it's brutally honest, it's gory, and it's extremely shocking. Great photography, stellar acting; the only thing missing here is a satisfying third act. It's all about the journey; not the destination.

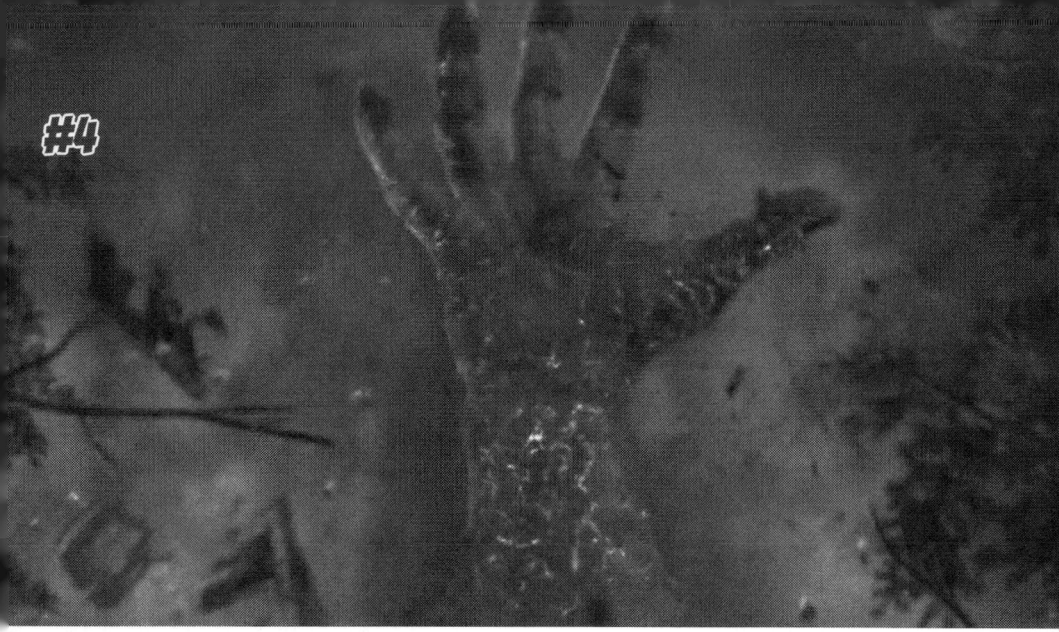

THE CABIN IN THE WOODS
2012

7/8

Five friends travel to a remote cabin where they get more than they bargained for.

The Cabin in the Woods is a parody of popular horror movies and horror movie tropes, including props, places and characters. Think of the desolated gas station, the mountain road, the remote cabin, the lake; all typically haunted by a killer with a mask and a weapon of choice. You get all the stereotypes, too; the dumb blonde, the jock, the scholar, the stoner and the virgin.

The casting isn't intuitive and character exposition, as extensive as it is, becomes futile because the Cabin the title refers to alters personalities. Clever! It's easy to spoil this film, considering the amount of twists it contains. The main thing you should know is that it was made for horror fans and, as such, it is a complete success. It is a surprise bag and it is unpredictable.

The creature design is well-done and, in some cases, very amusing. The creators manage to spoof big horror flicks while telling their own stories and, ultimately, without ruining the experience for the average movie-goer. Don't forget to blink, breath and hydrate yourself through the last act. It is an intense roller-coaster ride and it won't go easy on you!

DARK SHADOWS
2012

7/8

A dead vampire is brought back to life and returns to his ancestral home where he meets his dysfunctional descendants.

Johnny Depp, Michelle Pfeiffer, Helena Bonham Carter, Chloë Grace Moretz, Jonny Lee Miller, Eva Green, Jackie Earle Haley, Christopher Lee, Alice Cooper, scored by Danny Elfman and directed by Tim Burton; doesn't get much better than this. Sadly, the film didn't get the attention it deserves. It's one of Burton's underdogs. If you ask me, even to this day, the man has done no wrong.

It's based on the television soap opera of the same name. Sure, the humor doesn't always flow. The most recurrent gag has Depp's undead character dealing with the realities of 1972. Burton crafts a singular ambiance. The planets are aligned. This is a fabulous film! Most characters have secrets. Things aren't as they appear. It's one reveal after another.

The photography is superb. Visually, it doesn't get better than this. Dark Shadows isn't The Addams Family, but it's not far off. It's not as cute and friendly. Music plays an important role and is the source of several jokes. Most characters are cynical and sarcastic. There are no good guys, here. Everyone's selfish. Everyone's an asshole. Everyone's too cool for school.

BEST HORROR MOVIES OF 2013

EVIL DEAD

2013

8/8

Tricked into a week-end of rehab in a remote cabin by her friends, a girl in withdrawal believes she is surrounded by demons.

Technically second remake of a 1981 revolutionary cult classic, this movie has one of the strongest horror fan bases in history and a new generation of teenagers to seduce. The purists might bump on a few details, but none of the franchise's gimmicks have been overlooked and the movie looks like a million bucks. The gore effects are incredibly realistic and are torture even to the audience.

Bruce Campbell's Ash isn't part of the story, but his design and wit are found across the production. The performances range from forgettable to awesome, and it seems to be what the producers were after. This was also true of all previous films. Some actors hold back because the script wants them to until they get their special moment, at which point they unleash their true talent.

From photography to the narrative, every aspect of Evil Dead is calculated. It knows how to scare, disgust and make you jump, and does so with perfect timing. Humor is limited, much like the original Evil Dead. The biggest shift in tone between this and the first two is in the polish and the technology at hand. Nothing is left to chance. Expect twists and Easter eggs from beginning to end.

THIS IS THE END
2013

7/8

Six celebrities are stuck in a house after a series of devastating events destroyed the city.

This is the End is a horror comedy, with emphasis on "comedy". Seth Rogen, Jonah Hill, James Franco, Jay Baruchel; the all-star millennial jet set responsible for the most successful comedies of the last decade are gathered. Danny McBride, Craig Robinson, Michael Cera, and Emma Watson show up. This is as trendy as horror gets. It's your front seat to hilarity!

This is Seth Rogan and Even Goldberg's version of the apocalypse. Humor comes first, as always; we're both mocking and honoring horror films. It's one inside joke after another. The cast's chemistry speaks volume about how passionate everyone is. There is an unprecedented cohesion between the characters that you can't fake. It makes this film magical and extremely organic.

If you don't laugh your way through this thing, you're either missing the references or you're dead inside. This is the End is one of the funniest horror comedies ever made. The best joke of all? The end of the world, here, doesn't matter all that much. It's just an excuse to push a bunch of buffoons to their limits. Needless to say, the dialogue is phenomenal and only surpassed by the acting.

#3

CURSE OF CHUCKY

2013

7/8

A woman whose mother recently died suspects a mysterious doll might be responsible and a hazard to her niece.

We start with the assumption that the audience knows Chucky. The best thing about this one is that it embraces its root; a time when tongue in cheek horror was praised. Chucky used to be scary, but then got turned into a joke. Well, he thankfully inspires fear again. One of the main protagonists is a kid and we rediscover the evil doll again through a plot reminiscent of the original Child's Play.

The image is clean and crisp. The cinematography is studied and calculated, and many shots are set up in a complex fashion. The story manages to be both amusing and serious; at the same time and in alternation. The score is at time psychedelic, especially in moments of tension which the film excels at. Brad Dourif, the voice of Chucky, returns. The rest of the cast is motivated and performs well.

The main set is a beautiful mansion and the action mainly takes place on a rainy night. Along with a script that gives you all you wish for, the cutting-edge effects, animatronics included, return with a new upgraded but faithful look. The film's weaknesses can easily be overlooked, seeing how many surprises await you. Also, this new addition to the franchise has more than one twist in store...

OLDBOY
2013

7/8
A man imprisoned for twenty years then set free seeks answers and revenge.

The original Oldboy was a product of South Korea that didn't get the international credit it deserved, probably because of subtitles and the cultural barrier. Additionally, it was presumably considered too surreal and convoluted for a mainstream audience with a generally lower attention span. That said, the emotions stirred up by this masterpiece are universally compelling and relatable.

This is a tale of sadness, remorse and frustration disguised as a revenge story that doesn't exactly following the tropes of the subgenre. It is far from predictable but is filled with plot holes that it dares blame on surrealism. The film's biggest flaw is that its story progresses as we witness events the protagonists aren't aware of, yet they pickup on the invisible clues left for us.

We get the cream of actors and equivalent deliveries. The photography and the effects are impeccable. The eccentricities that created a buzz about the 2003 version are brought back and treated with respect, skill and innovation. Every technical challenge is reattempted and revised, then upped a notch. This film will make you face taboos in ways you can't imagine, unless you've seen the original...

CHEAP THRILLS
2013

7/8

A couple put a struggling family man and his friend through a series of increasingly twisted dares.

There aren't many movies like Cheap Thrills out there. It has an interesting gimmick that escalates continuously until it reaches dramatic proportions. It's all fun and games until someone gets punched in the face. The premise is fairly simple: two friends become involved in a game where they get paid to accomplish increasingly difficult challenges.

This whole mechanism orbits around four characters. First, there is Sara Paxton's character, whose beauty triggers the whole sequence of events. Then there's her boyfriend, played by David Koechner, who provides drugs and money. Pat Healy is the protagonist. He's broke and desperate. Ethan Embry, his friend, competes against him for cash. He's the asshole.

What first appears as a dark comedy turns into a horror movie by the third act. The script and the execution are A1. The actors are in complete control of perfectly well-cast characters. These characters are not deep or subtle, but they're entertaining, just like the story. Cheap Thrills asks a question we normally take lightly and hypothetically: how far are you ready to go and for how much?

BEST HORROR MOVIES OF 2014

LATE PHASES
2014

7/8
A veteran moves into a retirement community and is attacked by a werewolf.

For a werewolf movie to succeed, two criteria must be met. First, the beast itself must be photorealistic. Second, the transformation(s) must be explicit. Most werewolf films neglect these elements and perhaps shouldn't exist in the first place. Here, ten minutes in, we see our first werewolf. It starts with a silhouette through the curtains and it soon escalates into a full-blown attack.

The most peculiar aspect of Late Phases is that the second act takes place between two full moons, which creates a big gap where our beloved veteran works out and gears up, being the only character in the whole movie remotely aware of what's going on, for some reason. It's refreshing to see such an imperfect protagonist face his weaknesses with such determination.

He's blind, he's old, he's an asshole, but he has acute senses and he can use a gun and a shovel like no one can. You know how just about almost every lycanthrope movie has left you insatiate in the past? Well, be patient and give this one a chance. It will satisfy you beyond your wildest dreams. It is worth the wait. The protagonists are colorful and time with them is time well spent.

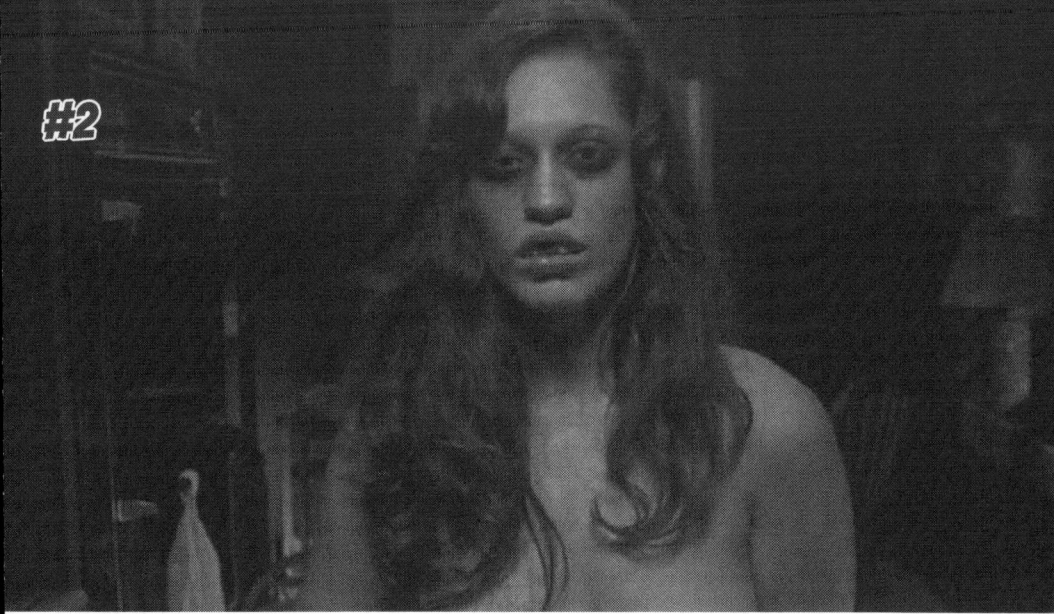

IT FOLLOWS
2014

7/8

After a sexual encounter, a young woman is followed by a supernatural entity that can take human forms.

This horror movie is about a monster whose modus operandi makes its victims feel alone and isolated, no matter how well surrounded they are. Consequently, the audience feels that way, too. Writer and director David Robert Mitchell is really good at setting an ambiance and sticking to it. Most of the day scenes are shot under a cloudy sky and it is very depressing.

But it's fitting, see, because this situation is hopeless. The first act can be shocking, as we understand the complexity of the main threat and how it pushes its victims to turn against their peers. In a nutshell, "it" is a supernatural sexual disease that moves from one partner to another. It is a monster that can take any human form. It follows you wherever you go, and it never gives up.

How creepy is that, considering you can't even afford to sleep? It Follows is one of the scariest movies ever made. It is also the kind of film that could generate countless sequels if they were done right. It makes the most out of its gimmick, yet it leaves us wanting more. The special effects are sparse but oh so effective. The budget was relatively small and that's never a problem.

TIME LAPSE
2014

6/8

Three friends discover a machine that takes pictures twenty-four hours into the future and use it for personal gain.

Time Lapse, in a nutshell, is about a machine that takes pictures in the future. It's less complicated than it sounds. This story is fascinating and not at all convoluted, considering the premise. The protagonists stick to one rule in order to avoid paradoxes: don't fuck with time. They figure that out once they find the previous owner dead and somehow mummified.

The movie takes unexpected turns to avoid stagnation, and generally for the best. This is one of the more user-friendly time travel films out there, but it may still divide the audience passed the halfway mark. It contains a few plot holes that do not pertain to time travel per say. For instance, who leaves their curtains open at all times, and why is this bookie so smart?

For everything unclear about Time Lapse, there is a myriad of mini subplots that drive the story in interesting directions, like that obsession to keep the death of the neighbor secret, or the lies and cuckolding, or the decision to make money off time travel, though that's been done time and again in film and literature. All in all, Time Lapse is a solid recommendation.

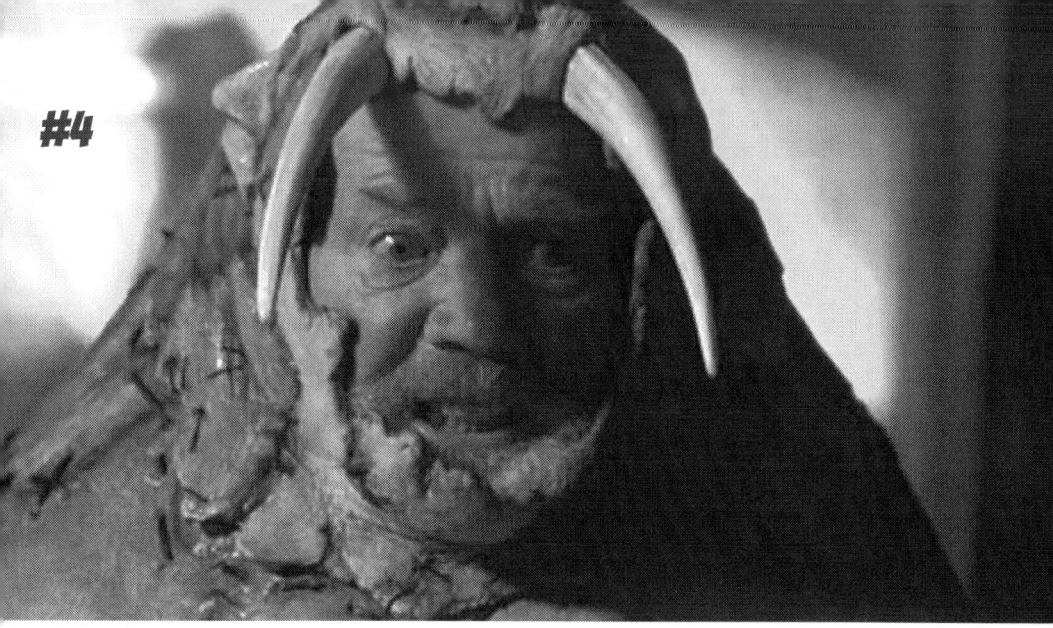

TUSK
2014

6/8
A podcast host is turned into a walrus by a mad man.

As funny and arrogant as Justin Long's character may be, and despite the fact that he gets turned into a walrus, this is Michael Parks' show. Parks relishes a singular type of dialogue where every word is replaced by a distant synonym and where every story told takes forever to conclude. His character's reasoning is circular, but he is half crazy so, for all we know, he may be making stuff up.

The script is chaotic for some reasons. First, Johnny Depp's character is basically a clown disguised as an investigator. He is unrecognizable and his acting is hysterical. Secondly, the film is half way between The Human Centipede and Misery. The walrus metamorphosis is funny, disgusting, but also extremely sad. Finally, Tusk vacillates between wide ranges of emotions, unable to find balance.

This is a horror comedy with humor so dark it seems written by sadists... drunken sadists! It is, in fact, a story improvised on writer and director Kevin Smith's podcast with a few adjustments. Tusk is meant to initiate a planned trilogy called the True North, where fun is made of Canadians, which they do a fine job of, here. Smith's cliches may be far-fetched but his caricatures are hilarious.

CLOWN
2014

6/8

A father puts on a clown suit for his son's birthday, only to realize it is cursed and won't come off.

Despite an evocative title, and while it is truly horrifying, Clown is not the quintessential killer buffoon movie. It's not just about an evil clown but a haunted costume, ultimately, that engulfs his wearer and transmutes him slowly then drives him crazy. This is not the clown your mom warned you about. He's much worse. His transformation is slow, painful, and disgusting.

The film goes in really dark places. It goes as far as making children potential victims, and it doesn't give them a special treatment. The clown costume comes with a dense mythos that would be too heavy in the hands of weak writers. On the contrary, in this case, it gives the movie depth. For a good while, we're not sure what kind of creature we are dealing with.

The actors are excellent. The camera is always where it needs to be. The script focuses on the right elements. This is storytelling at its best. I wouldn't call Clown a comedy, but it's a rapid fire of dark humor and sarcasm. Children dying horribly can be funny. Extreme gore can be hilarious. Clowns are hysterical. For all these reasons, this movie deserves to be seen.

BEST HORROR MOVIES OF 2015

THE FINAL GIRLS
2015

7/8
Four friends get pulled into a 1980s slasher and must avoid getting killed.

This slapstick comedy isn't afraid to get dramatic to get its point across, but 95% of it is delirious. It is fascinating and hysterical. It's a spoof of Friday the 13th, first and foremost, but it's also about a cyclic time loop, it's meta, and it's an unusual time travel movie. It's also claustrocore in its own way. Every second of this gem is fascinating and unprecedented.

The characters are a likable bunch, even the ones in the film within the film. They get our imaginations running wild. Adam Devine and Angela Trimbur are hilarious as the two dumbest 80's slasher flick stereotypes a writer could possibly come up with. The way the two realities merge is far-fetched, but it's better to roll with it, considering where the script takes us if we suspend our disbelief.

Billy Murphy's design is as close as possible to Jason Voorhees', and it's impressive how much the creators got away with. In this film, the killer comes second. The Final Girls is all about the survivors. This production nears perfection. The dialogue is right out of a stand-up comedian's mouth. Everything in the script feels calculated. This is an ode to horror movie fans.

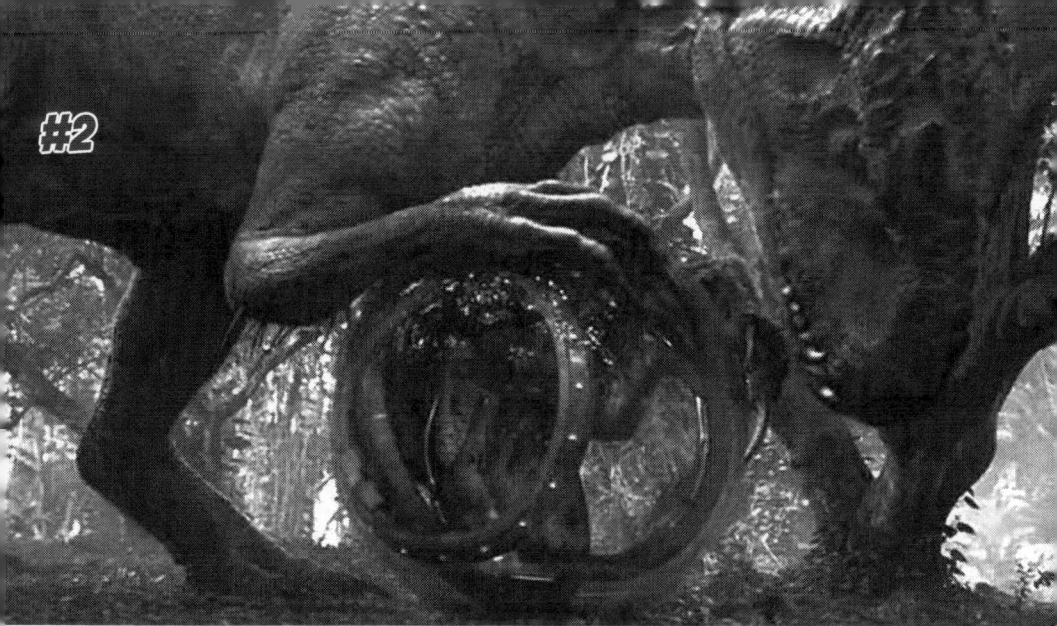

JURASSIC WORLD
2015

7/8

The owners of a theme park featuring genetically modified dinosaurs lose control of their installations.

This high budget sequel to a popular streak of movies aims higher than ever. It is a pimped out version of Jurassic Park on all levels. The action scenes are longer, the dinosaurs get more screen time and the 3-D is more convincing than before. The soundtrack is grandiose, always appropriate; tense during action scenes, scary in desperate moments and astonishing in times of contemplation.

Dinosaurs made out of practical effects are arguably more interesting than their CG counterpart, but the two animation techniques are difficult to tell apart, proof that we've come a long way since 1993's Jurassic Park. The landscapes are immense jaw-dropping painting-like scenes that contribute greatly to the immersion. A million elements come in place to make us feel we are part of the picture.

Two new deadly dinosaurs are introduced. On is aquatic, the Hainosaurus, and the other, Indominus Rex; a killing machine that uses camouflage, kills for fun and possesses a superior intelligence. Indominus is the main antagonist. A nice collection of dinosaurs then fill in the blank. The kids will love them! Jurassic World, all things considered, is just as good as the original. Don't miss out!

KRAMPUS

2015

7/8

A boy accidentally summons a demon before Christmas.

When it comes to Christmas horror, Krampus is as good as it gets. It starts as a tongue-in-cheek comedy poking fun at everything bad there is about the holidays, from kids fighting constantly to the bad side of the family, and joking avidly about capitalism, bad food, and even religion. As the story unfolds, we discover the more dramatic side of a script that only gets better with time.

The exposition is priceless. The best actors are given more prominent roles. We're talking Adam Scott, Toni Collette, David Koechner and Emjay Anthony, who all show a wide range of emotions. The most interesting aspect of Krampus is its supernatural element. It is extremely imaginative. The creature design is exactly what a child's mind would come up with, so why has no one attempted this before?

Snow, wreaths, colorful lights, holiday music, candles, presents, a Christmas tree; you get it all. Add to that a bunch of despicable characters who've probably been naughty all year long, and the "shadow of Santa Claus", and you're in for a horrific experience. The writers are not afraid to be politically incorrect and it pays off. Watch out for that second half; it's out of this world!

PATCHWORK
2015

7/8

Three women who go out partying one night find themselves stitched together in one body.

In Patchwork, three women are frankensteined together by a mad surgeon. This is easier said than done since we need the three leads to interact, somehow. A premise like this one has limitations, so the abomination, for lack of a better term, escapes, and tries to figure shit out to thicken the plot. This results in three undead chicks having discussions as if they were still distinct entities.

This is a small concept easily fleshed out when you start telling its various arcs anachronistically. Chapters are introduced with title cards. This accomplishes two things. First, we're thrown right in the action, from the get-go. Second, we end up caring for people we didn't initially know. Like its protagonists, this story is stitched together broadly. And it works.

The acting is particularly good, especially when taking into account the script's peculiarity. Tory Stolper plays the three-person hybrid. She does a great job with an unprecedented character. She does, after all, play several people at once. Kudos to the make-up department for making this as realistic as possible. They did an amazing job on her and on the gore.

KNOCK KNOCK
2015

7/8
A father helps two stranded young women who knock on his door.

Knock Knock is a straight man's wildest wet dream, that is, before it turns into his worst nightmare. One could say this script was written for them. Gay men and straight women will probably not relate with Keanu Reeves' character the same way. He's a pretty bad husband. It would be easily to spoil this film, but let's just say he manages to ruin Father's Day by cheating on his wife.

This is a simple story that evolves the way most thrillers do, with the hero trying to get away from an embarrassing situation. Eli Roth, master of horror, gives us yet another torture film, but this one hits close to home. Reeves makes a fatal mistake and pays the price. The two female antagonists are everything the script needs them to be: they make you horny, and then they scare you.

Whether you think cheating is acceptable or not, if you like old fashioned thriller, then this is for you. Are you kinky? Into BDSM? Fetishism, maybe? If so, you need to watch this. There are no safe words, here. There are no rules. There is nothing good awaiting Keanu Reeves' character passed the halfway mark. Knock Knock unravels the way classic thrillers do, but it's its own thing.

BEST HORROR MOVIES OF 2016

11.22.63

2016

8/8

A time traveler attempts to prevent John F. Kennedy's assassination.

Who has never felt the deep desire to fix today's problems yesterday; to go back in time and erase critical mistakes. The film explores this question more in-depth than Back to the Future did. 11.22.63 is easily one of the best time travelling stories ever adapted to screen. It's a mini-series, so it requires involvement, but every second is worth it. You should jump in head first!

11.22.63 is a science-fiction story and a supernatural drama. It contains horrific scenes, but in the midst of it evolves a touching love story. This is also one of Stephen King's most political tale, and one of his most mature work despite the colorful premise. In this mini-series, a time traveler; James Franco's character, attempts to prevent John F. Kennedy's assassination in 1963.

This feature is dialogue-oriented. Though not everyone is a big star, all actors are highly competent. Those who are reluctant to see James Franco in the protagonist's shoes will surely reconsider. He is amusing and extremely sympathetic. His character deserves to achieves his goals but fails at every step. You see, the past doesn't want to be changed. The past is the ultimate villain, in fact...

GHOSTBUSTERS
2016

7/8
Four women found a ghost hunting company.

The events in this remake take place 27 years after Ghostbusters 2, in what we presume is an alternate New York City. Instead of four males, we get four female Ghostbusters. The humor, much like the characters, is sometimes so dumb it is embarrassing. Mind you, this is the film's biggest flaw. Everything, here, is bigger and more colorful than what we are used to and it feels great!

All actors deserve a round of applause for keeping up with a script that is both dialogue and action heavy. We constantly alternate between humor, slapstick comedy, light horror and action. In the middle of all this are a bunch of cameos present to please the faithful fans. Like its predecessors, the film is accessible to all audiences, given they can take a couple of jump scares and fart jokes.

The first half will make you laugh and the second one will have your heart pumping. The last act is incredibly satisfying, high on emotions and big on special effects. It makes all the character exposition worthwhile. This remake is both an ode to the classic Ghostbusters films and a long overdue upgrade with digital effects instead of practical ones. The new generation of moviegoers will love it!

OUIJA: ORIGIN OF EVIL

2016

7/8

A mother and her daughters experiment with a Ouija board.

Compared to the first movie, Ouija: Origin of Evil doesn't always take two steps back every time it takes one step forward. It doesn't shy away from its own actions and it fully assumes the consequences of what it shows you. It always jumps to the next logical plot element no matter how crazy things get. This sometimes leads to repetition but not the kind you'd complain about.

But this film's best accomplishment, as the prequel of a much weaker production, is that it doesn't neglect its predecessor. It loosely ties in to 2014's Ouija despite how big a flop that was. The amount of terrorizing moments Ouija: Origin of Evil contains is a tour de force considering it isn't gory. It's more tragic than it is violent and it's more psychological than physical.

It's a period piece, too. It is set in the 1960s. What a smart move! The lack of technology and the slow lives of the protagonists create layers of eeriness. Ouija: Origin of Evil is not just about a haunted board game. It's a story about spirits, possession, possibly demons; you see, things are never fully explained and it's scarier that way. In fact, this is one of the scariest flicks out there!

DON'T BREATHE

2016

7/8

Three thieves break into the house of a blind man who isn't as helpless as he seems.

In Don't Breathe, a handicap is only a weakness if it doesn't make you a badass. Stephen Lang plays a war veteran who's simply defending his home and fortune against three bums. As it turns out, the thieves are the protagonists, and they're in big trouble. Silence is powerful, here. The man whose property they are trespassing on is blind, but quite resourceful.

Like him, the camera is highly dynamic, ominous and omnipresent. The editing is impeccable, and particularly when it comes to audio. The script is tight, despite the small story. Don't Breathe is a claustrocore film with no fluff, no filler, and, despite a slow pacing, no second is wasted on trivial plot details. As surreal as it appears, the film is strangely plausible.

Jane Levy and Dylan Minnette's characters easily outlive Daniel Zovatto's, who was predestined to die, with his shitty attitude and his lack of depth. Also, this movie, passed the halfway mark, introduces a key element that makes us reconsider everything we've seen; something so horrible that our attention gets shifted and everything we took for granted gets deconstructed and shuffled.

THE CONJURING 2
2016

7/8
Two ghost hunters attempt to exorcise a family's house.

This is one of the scariest movies you'll ever see. James Wan, writer and director, surpasses himself by polishing his style. He uses camera tricks he's perfected and loud noises to make us cringe and jump. This film contains one of the largest amounts of jump scares in horror movie history. It is relentless; a long roller-coaster ride. It simply won't let you breathe!

The picture mostly centers on one case of haunting and possession, but a couple of subplots orbit around it. We're basically dealing with a ghost, a spirit and a demon, which convolutes the story but prevents it from burning too slowly and having pacing issues. In other words, you might spend most of your time covering your face. There is always something horrible going on and tension never drops.

The actors are stellar; even the kids. The photography is textured, always controlled; never too light and never too dark. The camera movements are fluid and mathematically synchronized with the effects. You can't even tell what is practical and what is computer-altered. The only problem, here, is the procedural. Convenient conclusions to complex phenomena are pulled and turn out to be right.

BEST HORROR MOVIES OF 2017

IT
2017

8/8

A group of bullied kids band together against a shapeshifting demon clown.

Keep away from children! This film is not for them, despite the fact that all protagonists are tweens. They're young but they're in a horror movie and they're here to suffer. As such, they get beaten in the cruelest ways. For a while, the script opposes each child in the "losers' club" to Pennywise, one of the creepiest clowns in film history. He fucks with them then leaves, often interrupted.

Perfect sound, pacing, lighting, perfect acting and overall cinematography; It is nearly flawless. It is quite simply one of the best horror movies ever made, and, undoubtedly, one of the scariest. In comparison with the 1990 mini-series by the same title, everything, here, is more extreme, sad, scary and shocking. You get a bunch of solid jump scares that fool you even if you expect them.

Many special effects are computer generated and that's not really a problem. It's a style. Complaining about the abundance of compositing would be nitpicking. The characters' chemistry is representative of the actors' bounding on set. Their relationships are warm and compelling. The adults are all scums. This is the first part of a duology and it takes place in the 1980s.

CULT OF CHUCKY
2017

7/8
A possessed doll infiltrates a psychiatric hospital.

After you've gone through an opening so nerve-racking you just might swallow your tongue, you're transported to a sanitarium, of all places, where all the good stuff is about to take place. Like Curse of Chucky, this film centers on Fiona Dourif's character; Chucky's daughter, who's about the furthest thing there is from a stereotypical final girl.

Cult of Chucky is a fascinating mindfuck with more twists and turns than any of its predecessors. You won't see most surprises coming until they hit you right in the face. The murders are gory and look cool as hell. The photography surpasses all we've seen up to now. Chucky never looked so good and so alive. We can no longer tell how he is animated from shot to shot.

Don Mancini, writer, director and franchise owner, learned a lot from "Curse", the previous film. The last thing he wants is another Seed of Chucky. He follows Curse of Chucky's winning combination to a T: put the scares and the mystery first; the humor and the Easter eggs second. That being said, all Chucky movies should be watched in order. They are first and foremost made for fans.

ALIEN: COVENANT
2017

7/8
The crew of a colony ship discover an uncharted planet where danger awaits.

It seems, when it comes to criticizing this franchise, that Part 1, Alien, and Part 2, Aliens, are the only unanimous choices. 3 was too artsy. 4 didn't understand Ripley. The Alien vs. Predator films were too superficial for purists. You hear it all. And Prometheus got some fans mad. Well, perhaps Alien: Covenant will meet the franchise's lovers halfway. Yes, it might just be the right formula.

It has the type of procedural Alien had, but with Prometheus' flavour. It has guns and explosions, being reminiscent of Aliens, but it's also its own thing. It's well balanced. It's gory, tense; it can be slow and it can be larger than life. There are many surprises along the way; some you will see coming and some you won't. Like fireworks, it gets more intense the closer you get to the end.

Many scenes were specially crafted to reminisce about past installments. Some are right out of a slasher flick. Cyborgs are prominent. Xenomorphs make special appearances. They're modeled in 3-D but it allows realistic articulation. It makes them more agile than puppets have been in the past. We feel a strong influence from HR Giger, one of the men responsible for the original creature design.

KONG: SKULL ISLAND
2017

7/8

A team of scientists exploring an uncharted island are attacked by a variety of giant monsters.

A lot of money went into this and it wasn't wasted. John Goodman and Samuel L. Jackson are good indicators. They don't play characters that are easy to portray, and they give excellent performances regardless. Goodman is a government agent and Jackson a lieutenant colonel. This is a period piece taking place in 1973 and we're not sure why it matters.

Once passed the introduction, we spend all our time on Skull Island, a gorgeous but dangerous place. The scenery is sumptuous, and we can't tell how much was done digitally. The creatures look amazing. The camera is dynamic and equally immersive. The soundtrack is fitting, and the score is epic. There is some gore; just enough to get the story across.

The dialogue isn't always clever. Jackson gets the best lines, of course. There is a constant back and forth protagonist/antagonist switch between his team, the local tribe, the main protagonists, Kong and the ultimate enemies; the "really evil giant monsters". This is a little overwhelming, but it keeps the action going. All in all, this is one of the best King Kong movies out there.

GHOST STORIES
2017

7/8

A television personality who debunks supernatural myths investigates three cases of ghost manifestations.

You'll be completely sucked in from the first scene of the framing story onward. That story is interrupted three times; one for each segment, and it's relatively slow compared to your average horror anthology wraparound tale. First things first; the only obnoxious thing about this movie is its anxiogenic jump scares, and they kind of grow on you. Otherwise, Ghost Stories is nearly perfect.

All three stories share a common structure; they're all about men, alone, who are being haunted by ghosts. The first one is about a security guard inspecting a former asylum. The second one is about a young man who hits a demonic creature with his car, in the woods, at night. The last one is about a widower dealing with memories of a disastrous pregnancy.

Films like these are the reason some of us are scared of ghosts, late at night, alone. This story will follow you in the shower and in your bed. If you never believed in ghosts, now is the time. Ghost Stories doesn't take for granted that we've seen hundred of ghost stories. It's shot the way people who claim they've seen ghosts describe them. It's certainly not for the faint-hearted.

BEST HORROR MOVIES OF 2018

UPGRADE
2018

7/8

A quadriplegic technophobe receives an implant that grants him the strength to avenge his girlfriend's death.

Leigh Whannell has been offering us nothing but good movies for years, and Upgrade is no exception. It's different. It's a dark science-fiction action flick. It's a sinister take on the superhero movie. It's about a man who rejects technology in a near-future, and who must make a leap of faith in embracing it. It's a sad story, but sadness never lingers. We get rage instead, every step of the way.

Upgrade is extremely violent, but only when it's trying to make a point. The gore is there to satisfy us. Grey, the main protagonist, played by Logan Marshall-Green, is a suicidal man turned into a killing machine because vengeance is his last resort. The camera, when the implant takes over, becomes part of him and it almost feels like we're in his shoes.

As the voice inside his head explains, at one point, "If I cease to operate, you cease to move". The script is brilliant. It'll keep you guessing. You won't see half the twists coming and you won't guess how this film ends. One thing you can expect, though, is epic fights and speeding cars. There will be action, there will be suspense and there will be blood.

THE PREDATOR
2018

7/8
A young boy accidentally summons intergalactic hunters while manipulating alien technology and it's up to his father to save the day.

This film is everything fans of the Predator franchise could hope for, and even more. The pacing is tight, the special effects are badass, the actors are all talented and giving it all they have, the predator looks like a million bucks and, guess what, he brought friends. His friends come with spoilers, so let's leave it at that. The original score returns to send shivers down our spines.

The predator's gear, here, plays an important role. Alien technology in general is treated like some kind of puzzle to solve in order to assist humans against predators and to move the plot forward. Each of the Predator films, so far, has reinvented the franchise in their own way, and this new installment is no exception. It is one of the best sequels.

It takes place in space, in the sky, on the ground; in the forest and on the road. It is action-packed and extremely satisfying. It's an unusual combination of genres and it's ambitious. Some of the protagonists are nutcases, and they turn an otherwise serious film into a comedy. Yes, a comedy! It took a while, but they finally did Predator justice.

#3

JURASSIC WORLD: FALLEN KINGDOM
2018

7/8

Several dinosaurs are rescued from an island threatened by an active volcano.

This is a sequel of Jurassic World, which in return is a sequel of Jurassic Park. This time, the military is up to no good and you know where this is going from the moment you see them on screen. The script is compartmentalized. We get a short intro, with Jeff Goldblum, who's only here to tease us, then a segment on the island during a volcano eruption, and everything else happens in a manor.

The volcano sequence and the third act are breath-taking. They're some of the best moments in the franchise. Ted Levine is here because we need someone to hate. Bryce Dallas Howard looks more human, this time around, and Chris Pratt beats up bad guys. There are many brilliant moments of extreme tension skillfully written and directed. Nothing is left to chance.

Am I the only one who isn't crying, here? Half these dinosaurs would bite her head off if she let them, and Bryce's character sheds a tear every time one of them bites the dust? Fallen Kingdom is an amazing film, but it has a political agenda. It is pro-environment and anti-capitalist. It's not subtle. It's not reasonable. It's immature. Other than that, kudos!

PUPPET MASTER: THE LITTLEST REICH
2018

7/8

Puppets gathered for auction at a convention are magically animated and kill everyone.

Puppet Master: The Littlest Reich is very loyal and respectful of the Puppet Master franchise but does things better and differently. It reinvents itself in every way possible while upholding most of the mythos. Something needed to be done because this series was going nowhere interesting. This new addition doesn't conflict with previous films and feels like both a sequel and a remake.

Continuity is maximized and there are no plot holes, except perhaps Andre Toulon's arc, which doesn't make a lot of sense. The whole Nazi versus Jewish element is kind of heavy, but it's been hindering these movies since the beginning and it must exist. The Littlest Reich has, by far, the best puppetry we've seen. The actors are excellent, no matter how significant their part is.

This mostly takes place in a hotel. It is where it all started, after all, and Puppet Master purists will appreciate it. The best thing about this movie is that the puppets are evil, so expect a slasher and a significant body count. There are boobs and there is sex, in case you wondered. The creators left nothing to chance. In fact, this may very well be the best Puppet Master movie to date.

THE MEG
2018

7/8
A team of scientists are attacked by a megalodon.

Say what you will about The Meg; it's one of the best shark movies out there. It's not much of an accomplishment, considering how crappy most of these are, but there is a demand and this film meets expectations. When it comes to storytelling, The Meg may be fast-food, but it's expensive fast-food. It's a blockbuster you won't remember a year from now, so enjoy it while it's hot.

Jason Statham is the alcoholic action hero, Rainn Wilson the comic relief, Cliff Curtis is just another face, Bingbing Li plays a fervent oceanographer, and Ruby Rose, well, she's there to respond and react. In both cases, she models more than she acts. A lot of time is spent underwater, and these shots always look great. Some or most of it is computer-generated, but who cares?

The writers make the typical submarine mumbo jumbo fascinating, somehow, but the dialogue isn't brilliant. The characters aren't really fleshed out, but the actors make it work. This is an action film and a light comedy, something Jaws wasn't. You get breath-taking action sequences and you get them quite often. The pacing is tight. The score is exciting. The finale is hilarious!

BEST HORROR MOVIES OF 2019

IT: CHAPTER TWO
2019

8/8

Twenty-seven years after defeating a supernatural being, six friends are reunited to kill it once and for all.

This is the kind of film non-horror movie fans think we watch all the time. If only they knew! A phenomenon like It: Chapter 2 happens once every year, at best, and is just as good as Part 1 was. The casting is brilliant. It takes a while to figure out who's who, between the cast of Part 1 and their adult counterpart, but it eventually sinks in. I ended up connecting with everyone in this.

There are several flashbacks, so the original cast reprise their roles. Pennywise returns, too, of course, to fuck with everyone's mind and kill a few. There are genuinely creepy moments that will make you swallow your tongue. The creature design is unbelievable. This is a horror fan's wet dream come true. I was one with this movie and never wanted it to end.

This story constantly came full circle. When we think of what a quintessential horror movie is, this is the one that comes to mind. The special effects are out of this world. There are jump scares at every turn. There's a bit of every horror trope in this, but with a special touch that makes them unique. Legendary casting! Amazing cinematography! What a great flick!

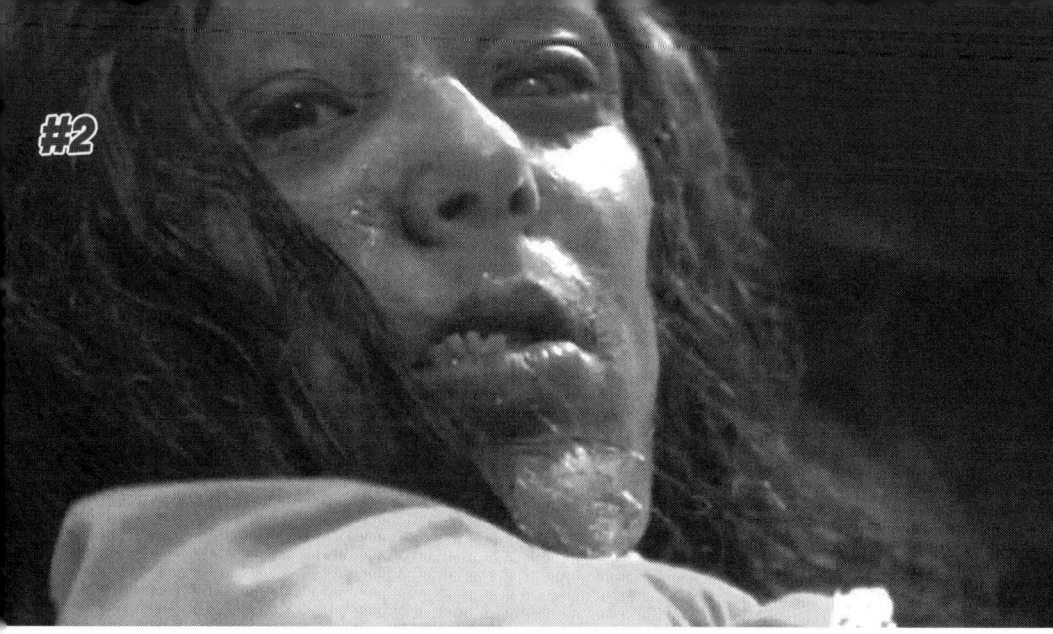

PET SEMATARY
2019

7/8
A doctor and his family relocate to a rural town, next to a haunted cemetery.

Whether or not you're familiar with King's novel and the first installment of this franchise will account for a lot in this experience. There are significant changes made to a story that arguably didn't need any. The intent was to be unpredictable, of course. This remake, and re-imagining, has something the other films lacked: a massive budget. For the most part, they spent that money wisely.

Jason Clarke carries this film on his shoulders, Amy Seimetz plays the most sympathetic character and her backstory is terrifying, John Lithgow is great as always, but the revelation, here, is child actress Jeté Laurence, for reasons what will remain unspoiled. Also, whoever trained and directed that cat deserves a pat on the back, and so does the cat, in fact.

The film's first mission is to give us a heart attack. It's scary as hell. That said, hadn't the editing been so tight, this could've been more effective. Its second mission is to keep us guessing. I sure didn't see those plot twists coming. Its final mission is to make us cry. This film is cruel, stressful, but first and foremost, it's incredibly sad. It's a sinister story we can all related to.

BRIGHTBURN

2019

7/8

A child from another world uses his superpowers for evil.

I wonder just how far you can take an homage until it becomes copyright infringement and without getting sued for it. Brightburn is basically Superman's origin story with an evil Clark Kent adapted as a horror thriller. This is a fast-paced ride that escalates quickly. The editing is tight. The writers have a lot to say and the director has a lot to show.

Jackson A. Dunn plays Brandon, the young alien supervillain; Elizabeth Banks and David Denman his adoptive parents. Brandon's superpowers are revealed early on. He has super strength, super speed, heat vision, invincibility, telekinesis, he can levitate and fly, and he gets super pissed at people. His murders are explicit and extremely gory. Some might make you look away.

The special effects are powerful and convincing, the story is exciting, the actors are excellent, and so is the dialogue. This is great casting. Whatever the budget was, it was obviously spent in the right places. This is, simply put, one of the best evil kid movies out there. It's certainly one of the most extreme. Brightburn deserves a sequel for all kinds of reasons.

DOCTOR SLEEP
2019

7/8

A man with psychic powers must protect a child with similar abilities from a cult of wizards.

How do you follow up with what is, arguably, the best horror movie ever made? The Shining may one day be surpassed, but, as of 2019, it's the most epic and quintessential supernatural thriller there is. Prove me wrong! Doctor Sleep's writer and director Mike Flanagan reconstructed some of the most iconic scenes of 1980's The Shining. He cast lookalikes and built almost identical sets.

Doctor Sleep is, first and foremost, the story of energy vampires who kidnap people, kill them, and absorb their "shine". This isn't a spoiler, but pretty much everything else is. The film is a succession of surprises. This plotline is more about the "shining" than its predecessor was, and a lot of the action happens in people's heads. This element from the novel was certainly hard to adapt.

We can feel how busy Flanagan is reaching the milestones of the original material. He wants to pay homage to King's book, while reminiscing about 1980's The Shining. There are things Kubrick didn't explore, and this is where Doctor Sleep comes full circle. This movie probably isn't what you expect but give it a chance. That third act will send shivers down your spine.

THE SHED
2019

7/8
Something dangerous hides in a teenager's tool shed.

Stan's environment is hostile: bullies, angry cop, abusive grandfather. His day is about to get much worse; there's a thing in the shed. No one comes out of there alive. This being a feature-length film, of course things escalate, but the plot keeps its small scope. The script appeared straightforward, and I kept hoping it would stay that way. Whatever hid in the shed needed to stay there.

The Shed is a Goosebumps episode gone wrong. It has a great hook and it lives up to expectations. It gives you exactly what you want. Sure, it's predictable, but it's an emotional outlet. It still manages to build tension, mystery, and excitement. How many times have you rented a movie with a killer gimmick and a sexy title, only to be let down and betrayed by the second act? Won't happen here!

What you see is what you get. This isn't arthouse. It's not pretentious. Despite its basic script, it's not easy to classify either. It's hard to tell what kind of monster we are dealing with, which makes the film more frightening. This movie won't let you down. There are no slow moments, there are surprises at every turn, and the last act is bonkers.

FOR MORE HORROR-THEMED BOOKS, VISIT

WWW.TERROR.CA

Printed in Great Britain
by Amazon